GALATIANS

THROUGH

COLOSSIANS

AND

PHILEMON

WESLEY BIBLE STUDIES

wesleyan
PUBLISHING HOUSE
wphstore.com
Indianapolis, Indiana

CONTENTS

INTRODUCTION
Guidelines for a Healthy Body

As an old year grinds to an end and a new one dawns, ads promoting better health multiply. We get bombarded with ads about weight loss programs, gym memberships, dietary supplements, and spa treatments. The healthcare programs, products, and memberships may be worth the cost, but when all is said and done, simple guidelines for a healthy body remain the same: eat properly, rest adequately, and exercise regularly.

Throughout this study, we will find significant guidelines that make a healthy church body, particularly in terms of the church you attend. Here are a few of those guidelines.

MAINTAIN A PROPER
RELATIONSHIP WITH CHRIST

Christ is the head of the church. He created all things, sustains all things, and supplies all we need for a life that pleases God. Love and forgiveness flow from Him. He serves as the supreme example of humility and devotion to the Father's will. When a body of believers honors Christ as Lord and stays close to Him, it will be strong, active, and energetic.

MAINTAIN A PROPER RELATIONSHIP
WITH FELLOW BELIEVERS

It isn't always easy to get along with some believers, especially if they have offended us. However, Paul highlighted the need to forgive in his letter to Philemon. Recognizing that God forgave us is key to forgiving others, and forgiveness contributes to good health in any body of believers.

MAINTAIN GOOD VISION

Maintaining good vision is essential to good health, so we regularly visit the eye doctor. In his letter to the Philippians, Paul testified that he was reaching for the goal of the prize of the high calling in Christ Jesus. Obviously, his eye was on that important goal and not on the allurements of the world.

WALK WITH GOD EVERY DAY

Walking is an excellent form of exercise that costs nothing, yet it improves our cardiovascular system, tunes our muscles, helps us maintain good balance, and even wards off depression. In this study, we will learn to walk in step with the Holy Spirit and discover that doing so brings many benefits into our lives.

USE THE RESOURCES GOD HAS FOR YOU

Only a foolish person would buy a membership in a gym and then simply look at the gym's equipment. The equipment is designed to be used for a beneficial workout. Similarly, God has supplied us with the equipment we need to be strong. His Spirit is always available to help us live for Christ. Further, we can wield the sword of the Spirit, the Word of God, as an effective weapon. All the while, prayer acts as an unfailing supply line to keep God's resources flowing to us.

During this study, apply what you learn to your daily thoughts and actions. Share what you learn with other believers and pray for one another. Expect your personal spiritual health and the health of your corporate body of believers to thrive.

1

KEEPING IN STEP WITH THE SPIRIT

Galatians 5:16–26

The Spirit-filled life must produce fruit.

A soldier's proud parents watched his unit march along a parade route. "Look, John," the mother said, beckoning to her husband. "Everyone's out of step except our son."

Staying in step is important to the military and also to the walk of faith. When moral and spiritual corruption blanketed the pre-flood world, Enoch walked with God (Gen. 5:24). Like Enoch, we live in evil times, but we can walk with God by staying in step with the Spirit. This study makes clear that if we stay in step with the Spirit, our lives will display the fruit of the Spirit.

COMMENTARY

Paul wrote Galatians to "the churches in Galatia" (1:2). It seems that Paul had founded these churches himself (1:8–9; 4:19–20). The book of Acts records Paul making visits to this area on his first three missionary journeys (Acts 13:14—14:25; 16:1–6; 18:23).

A group called "Judaizers" insisted that Gentile Christians should be circumcised and observe the Jewish religious traditions (Acts 15:1). These zealots had thrown the Galatians into confusion (Gal. 1:8). Some of the Gentile Christians must have been persuaded to leave the gospel of Christ and submit to the law as the means of salvation (1:6; 3:1–5; 4:8–11; 5:7–8). Paul wrote to correct this error and bring them back to Christ (5:1–6).

Paul abruptly introduced the problem in the first ten verses of chapter 1. He then provided a defense of his credentials as an apostle in 1:11—2:21. Paul gave a striking contrast between salvation by faith in Jesus Christ and salvation by obeying the law (3:1—4:31). The final two chapters outline the way we are to live by faith—"the only thing that counts is faith expressing itself through love" (5:6).

In Galatians 5:1–12, Paul emphasized the freedom we have in Christ. We are God's sons and daughters by faith instead of being slaves to the law. In 5:13–26, Paul insisted that freedom from the law is not a license "to indulge the sinful nature" (5:13). Our freedom's goal is to "keep in step with the Spirit" (5:25) as "we serve each other in love" (5:13).

Live By the Spirit (Gal. 5:16–18)

In Romans, Paul condemned one of the objections the Judaizers raised against the gospel. "Why not say—as we are being slanderously reported as saying and as some claim that we say—'Let us do evil that good may result'? Their condemnation is deserved" (Rom. 3:8). The legalists believed the only way to receive God's approval was to earn it through the "human effort" of obeying the law (Gal. 3:3). In their eyes, freedom from the law could only mean a license to sin. Paul refused to cave in to their either/or assessment (Rom. 6:1–2, 14–18).

Paul avoided the extreme of legalism while shunning the extreme of using grace as a license to sin. He called the Galatians to enjoy their freedom from the law without giving in to the sinful nature (Gal. 5:13). **Live by the Spirit, and you will not gratify the desires of the sinful nature** (v. 16). **The sinful nature** or "flesh" (KJV, NASB, RSV, NKJV) is a selfish, self-reliant attitude that pursues its own goals in rebellion against God. It is the natural cause of the lifestyle that takes pride in human achievements and religious accomplishments. The desires of the sinful nature produce either legalism or licentiousness.

WORDS FROM WESLEY

Galatians 5:16

Now "whosoever abideth in him, sinneth not"; "walketh not after the flesh." The flesh, in the usual language of St. Paul, signifies corrupt nature. In this sense he uses the word, writing to the Galatians, "The works of the flesh are manifest" (Gal. 5:19); and a little before, "Walk in the Spirit, and ye shall not fulfill the lust" (or desire) "of the flesh" (5:16). To prove which, namely, that those who "walk by the Spirit," do not "fulfill the lusts of the flesh," he immediately adds, "For the flesh lusteth against the Spirit; and the Spirit lusteth against the flesh, (for these are contrary to each other), that ye may not do the things which ye would." (WJW, vol. 5, 88)

So, **the sinful nature** always **desires what is contrary to the Spirit** because it seeks to find satisfaction or salvation on its own. At the same time, **the Spirit** desires **what is contrary to the sinful nature** because He seeks to bring us to God through faith in Christ. **The sinful nature** and **the Spirit are in conflict with each other** (v. 17) because one seeks to elevate itself, while the other points us to the only One who can raise us up.

The only way to conquer the sinful nature is to live or walk by the Spirit. When you live by the Spirit, **you do not do what you want** (v. 17), that is, you surrender your selfish plans and goals to His will. **But**, remember, **if you are led by the Spirit, you are not under law** (v. 18). You are not trying to gain God's acceptance by slavish observance of the law. In fact, when you live by the Spirit you will fulfill the law of love (5:6, 14).

WORDS FROM WESLEY
Galatians 5:17

"But was he not then freed from all sin, so that there is no sin in his heart?" I cannot say this; I cannot believe it; because St. Paul says the contrary. He is speaking to believers, and describing the state of believers in general, when he says, "The flesh lusteth against the Spirit, and the Spirit against the flesh: These are contrary the one to the other" (Gal. 5:17). Nothing can be more express. The apostle here directly affirms that the flesh, evil nature, opposes the Spirit, even in believers; that even in the regenerate there are two principles, "contrary the one to the other." (WJW, vol. 5, 147)

Acts of the Sinful Nature (Gal. 5:19–21)

The acts of the sinful nature are obvious (v. 19). The results of living under its control are undeniable. These acts seem to flourish in a legalistic environment. The law not only defines sin for us, but the sinful nature uses it to arouse immoral desires in us (Rom. 7:7–11). The law is powerless to make us right with God because it is undermined by the sinful nature (Rom. 8:3).

The acts of the sinful nature are listed in four groups. The first group contains sensual sins. **Sexual immorality** refers to sexual acts outside of monogamous, heterosexual marriage. **Impurity** covers all kinds of sexual degradation. **Debauchery** involves being controlled by passions and desires (Gal. 5:19). This act of the sinful nature is unrestrained and shocking even to pagans.

The second group contains spiritual sins. **Idolatry** raises created things above the Creator. **Witchcraft** is sorcery (v. 20). Both directly engage humans with the forces of evil.

The third grouping deals with interpersonal relationships. **Hatred** is the opposite of the love summarized in the law (v. 14). It is hostility toward others. **Discord** alludes to arguments based on selfish competition. **Jealousy** is the desire to have what others have. **Fits of rage** involve outbursts of anger. **Selfish ambition** desires to rule over others so they can meet our needs. **Dissensions** are differences of opinion that cause individuals to stand apart from others. **Factions** are disagreements that have descended into dislike (v. 20). **And envy** is another selfish response to the good fortune of others (v. 21). Whereas jealousy wants what others have, envy simply resents the fact that others have anything at all. Envy only wants others to lose what they have.

The final group involves the loss of restraint. **Drunkenness** takes away a person's inhibitions. In **orgies** or "carousing" intoxication removes all sense of right and wrong from a whole group of individuals. The list could go on with **the like** (v. 21), but Paul has made his point: The acts of the sinful nature do not improve our standing with God. They only lead to destruction (6:8). In fact, **Those who live** (persist in living) according to the sinful nature **will not inherit the kingdom of God** (5:21).

The Fruit of the Spirit (Gal. 5:22–24)

Just as an apple can be red, tart, round, shiny, and smooth, **the fruit of the Spirit** (v. 22) is the singular result of His work in our lives. The Spirit produces the fruit in us by convicting us of not believing in Jesus and not acting like Him and by convincing us that judgment is coming (John 16:5–11). The Spirit also transforms and renews our minds so we can know God's will (Rom. 12:1–2). The result is that the ways we think, act, talk, and relate to others become more like Christ.

The fruit of the Spirit is love (Gal. 5:22). Love is an unconquerable desire for another person's good. It is an act of the will determining to work for someone's benefit no matter what the cost or response. Love was demonstrated for us on the cross. **The fruit of the Spirit is . . . joy** (v. 22), which is based on knowing God. Joy is independent of our circumstances. The book of Philippians is a call to rejoice, but Paul was in a Roman prison when he wrote it. **The fruit of the Spirit is . . . peace** (v. 22), which comes from knowing God is in control. He will always care for us. This outlook on love, joy, and peace is completely beyond the sinful nature.

The fruit of the Spirit also impacts our relationships. **The Spirit** produces **patience** (v. 22) or "long-suffering" (KJV). This is the behavior of one who refuses to seek revenge. It is a matter of bearing "with each other and [forgiving] whatever grievances you may have against one another" (Col. 3:13). **The fruit of the Spirit is . . . kindness** and **goodness** (Gal. 5:22) that are like the two sides of a coin. Kindness always seeks to help those in need. Goodness is willing to confront evil and sin when necessary. **The fruit of the Spirit is . . . faithfulness** (v. 22), which means trustworthy and reliable. The sinful nature cannot imagine relating to others like this.

WORDS FROM WESLEY

Galatians 5:22–23

The immediate fruit of the Spirit, ruling in the heart, are "love, joy, peace, bowels of mercies, humbleness of mind, meekness, gentleness, long-suffering." And the outward fruit are, the doing good to all men; the doing no evil to any; and the walking in the light— a zealous, uniform obedience to all the commandments of God.

By the same fruit shall you distinguish this voice of God, from any delusion of the Devil. That proud spirit cannot humble thee before God. He neither can nor would soften thy heart, and melt it first into earnest mourning after God, and then into filial love. It is not the adversary of God and man that enables thee to love thy neighbour; or to put on meekness, gentleness, patience, temperance, and the whole armour of God. He is not divided against himself, or a destroyer of sin, his own work. (WJW, vol. 5, 122)

The fruit of the Spirit improves our powers of self-discipline. It involves **gentleness** (v. 23), which is the strength to be angry at the right time, for the right reason, and in the right way. Gentleness is power under control to help others. **The fruit of the Spirit is . . . self-control** (vv. 22–23). That is the mastery of all our desires. The sinful nature always enslaves us by elevating our desires to the level of master. Only the Spirit and not the law can set us free.

Against such things there is no law (v. 23) because they are all facets of love. And "the entire law is summed up in a single command: 'Love your neighbor as yourself'" (v. 14). No commandments against sinful behavior could ever produce these holy attitudes and actions. They are most certainly the fruit of the Spirit.

In Step with the Spirit (Gal. 5:24–26)

Those who belong to Christ Jesus have crucified the sinful nature with its passions and desires (v. 24). Christians who have believed "the gospel [of] a righteousness from God" receive "a righteousness that is by faith" and not by human efforts to keep the law (Rom. 1:17; 3:21–24). Those who belong to Christ Jesus "know that all of us who were baptized into Christ Jesus were baptized into his death" (Rom. 6:3). They are dead to sin and must begin to live like it (Rom. 6:11–14).

We live by the Spirit (Gal. 5:25) in view of the fact that we have been raised to a new kind of life in Christ (Rom. 6:4–10). Therefore we should **keep in step with the Spirit** (Gal. 5:25). We need to follow His directions in all that we think, say, and do. He will guide us to "serve one another in love" (5:13). Loving words and deeds will make sure we do **not become conceited, provoking** those we consider beneath us **and envying** those we think are better than we are (v. 26).

DISCUSSION

If a person tried to swim across the Atlantic Ocean, his or her best attempt would fall short. Similarly, if a Christian attempts to lead a holy life in his or her own strength, failure will ensue. Fortunately, God wants every Christian to succeed, and He has made it possible to do so.

1. How do you define *legalism*? Why do you agree or disagree that legalism is common among Christians?

2. Why should Christians not depend on law-keeping for victory over sin?

3. Why do you agree or disagree that many Christians seem complacent about the works of the flesh?

4. The Holy Spirit produces Christlike traits in those who walk in the Spirit. How well are you exhibiting Christlike traits? If the fruit of the Spirit is not clearly evidenced in your life, will you determine to walk in the Spirit on a daily basis?

5. Joy is a quality that is included in the fruit of the Spirit. Have you noticed that legalistic people seldom, if ever, manifest joy? Why do they lack joy? Are joy and happiness identical? If not, how does joy differ from happiness?

6. If a Christian is constantly impatient with people or difficult circumstances, is he or she in step with the Holy Spirit? Explain.

7. Why is it significant that love heads the list of qualities associated with the fruit of the Spirit?

PRAYER

God, please release us from the bondage of trying to live by the law. Give us the freedom that comes from living in the Spirit's guidance and power.

2

FILLED WITH GOD AND HIS LOVE

Ephesians 3:14–21

The meaning of life is to know God and be filled with His love.

A young boy stood beside his dad at the top of Pikes Peak. He pointed far to the east, then to the west, then to the south, and finally to the north. For a moment he stood motionless and looked very studious. Suddenly, he turned in a complete circle with his arms extended to each horizon. "Just think, Dad," he exclaimed, "God's love is bigger than all of this."

When we pray for other Christians, do we confine our prayers to their physical and material needs? Those needs are important, but shouldn't we also pray that all of us will gain a deeper understanding of God's love? This study challenges us to grasp the many dimensions of His love.

COMMENTARY

With verse 14, Paul resumed the prayer he began in Ephesians 3:1. As Paul began to utter his prayer in 3:1, God broke into the conversation with a revelation of His purposes that was too wondrous to keep to himself. Now, in response to that, he offered a prayer filled with depth of understanding of God's will for the church. In 3:12, he assured his readers, "In him and through faith in him we may approach God with freedom and confidence." For this reason, Paul now approached the Father in prayer.

Paul's Prayer for the Church (Eph. 3:14–15)

Even though Paul has already contended that believers may approach the Father with "freedom and confidence" (3:12), such an approach is never to be without great humility. For the Jews, it was customary to stand in prayer except in cases of great emotion or earnestness. Solomon knelt during his stirring prayer of dedication for the temple in 1 Kings 8:54; Jesus knelt in prayer in the garden of Gethsemane the night before His crucifixion (Luke 22:41); Stephen's dying prayer was uttered on his knees (Acts 7:60). Here, too, in Ephesians 3:14, Paul said, **I kneel before the Father**, indicating the utmost humility, submission, solemnity, and emotion of this prayer.

WORDS FROM WESLEY
Ephesians 3:14, 16–19

Prayers for entire sanctification; which, were there no such thing, would be mere mockery of God. Such, in particular, are, (1) "Deliver us from evil"; or rather, "from the evil one." Now, when this is done, when we are delivered from all evil, there can be no sin remaining. (2) "Neither pray I for these alone, but for them also which shall believe on me through their word; that they all may be one; as thou, Father, art in me, and I in thee, that they also may be one in us: I in them, and thou in me, that they may be made perfect in one" (John 17:20, 21, 23). (3) "I bow my knees unto the Father of our Lord Jesus Christ—that he would grant you—that ye, being rooted and grounded in love, may be able to comprehend, with all saints, what is the breadth, and length, and depth, and height; and to know the love of Christ, which passeth knowledge, that ye might be filled with all the fullness of God" (Eph. 3:14, 16–19). (4) "The very God of peace sanctify you wholly; and I pray God your whole spirit and soul and body be preserved blameless unto the coming of our Lord Jesus Christ" (1 Thess. 5:23). (WJW, vol. 8, 295)

Paul used a deliberate play on words in these first two verses. He prayed to the Father in 3:14, and used a similar word in 3:15

when he mentioned the **whole family**, which literally means any father-headed group, referring to a family, tribe, or nation. But this family is unique in that it is composed of those **in heaven and on earth** (v. 15). Paul was no longer speaking about just his Christian readers; he was referring to the church universal—all those who have been part of God's family for all time, both those presently with the Lord and those still alive. There is a oneness expressed in Paul's prayer—only together with the saints that have gone before us do we truly constitute God's church. Together we are "fellow citizens with God's people and members of God's household" (2:19).

Paul's supplication for the church is threefold. Each request begins with a Greek word that means "so that." Though not always translated in the English, Paul used this word in 3:16, 18, and 19.

Prayer for Strength (Eph. 3:16–17)

Paul's first request was for God to **strengthen you with power** (v. 16). The word translated **power** means "the ability to do." Paul's desire was that the church be empowered to do what God has called it to do, recognizing that the work of the church can never be accomplished by human effort. Earlier he had written that God has an "incomparably great power for us who believe" (1:19). He later encouraged them to "be strong in the Lord and in his mighty power" (6:10). This is a keynote with Paul. Whatever God has called an individual to do or a local church to accomplish, He will empower them to do.

Notice, though, that this power comes **through his Spirit in your inner being** (3:16). It is not always an outer ability we need, but an inner strength that will keep us faithful to the task when the going gets tough. As we allow the Spirit to work in and through us, we can say with Paul, "Therefore we do not lose heart. Though outwardly we are wasting away, yet inwardly we are being renewed day by day" (2 Cor. 4:16). And God strengthens our inner beings **out of his glorious riches** (Eph. 3:16), out of His unlimited divine resources that can never be exhausted.

Paul's prayer that they be strengthened was for a purpose: **so that Christ may dwell in your hearts through faith** (v. 17). At first glance, it would appear that Christ dwells in our individual hearts (which includes the entire personality, mind, and will) through faith. The word **dwell** is in the present continuous tense, indicating a constantly maintained experience. Paul wrote that if a person doesn't have the Spirit of Christ living within, that individual doesn't belong to Christ (Rom. 8:9). And having the Spirit necessarily involves obedience: We must walk by the Spirit and be led and controlled by the Spirit. Though Christ dwells in our hearts by faith, a constant, obedient response is vital to maintaining that relationship. Our faith is not just intellectual; it expresses itself in love toward God and others. We are to be **rooted and established in love** (Eph. 3:17). Like a tree, we are to have deep roots in the soil of love. God's love for us should overflow and be evidenced in our love for others.

But there is another way of looking at verse 17. Instead of referring to the individual Christian life, Paul may have had the entire body of Christ in view. In 2:22, speaking of the church (members of God's household), he wrote, "And in him you too are being built together to become a dwelling in which God lives by his Spirit." The entity of the corporate church is a grand mystery. Somehow, when we gather together as the people of God (individuals strengthened and indwelt by the Spirit), Christ's presence dwells with us in a unique way, in a manner not possible individually. The church then is to be established in love, sharing the love of Christ with a lost and needy world and living in corporate obedience to the commands of God.

Prayer for Understanding (Eph. 3:18)

Paul realized that this concept of love is a hard one to comprehend, so his second request for these Christians (individually and as a church) was that they have the power **to grasp how wide and long and high and deep is the love of Christ** (v. 18). Unlike our earthly, limited views of human love, Christ's love is too large to be confined by measurements. But Paul wanted them to understand this love **together with all the saints** (v. 18). It is only as part of the church that we can ever truly grasp the many dimensions of God's love. As we gather together to hear the exposition of God's Word, to participate in the singing of His praises, and to listen to testimonies of God's gracious love to others in their unique situations, we gain an ever-increasing understanding of how immense that love really is. From our own limited perspectives, it is difficult, if not impossible, to truly grasp the extent of God's love.

Prayer for Love (Eph. 3:19)

Paul didn't want them to merely understand God's love intellectually; his prayer was that they would **know this love that surpasses knowledge** (v. 19). They were to know it intimately and experientially. The great danger we face, both individually and as a church, is that Christ's love becomes academic, with no fresh outpourings or expressions to the world around us. While Paul wanted them to know this love, he also realized that it is unknowable; that is, it is too deep for the mind to imagine or for human language to express. And yet, it is possible to know the unknowable if Christ dwells in us (see 1 Cor. 2:9–10).

WORDS FROM WESLEY
Ephesians 3:18-19

That being rooted and grounded—That is, deeply fixed, and firmly established *in love, ye may comprehend*—So far as a human mind is capable, *what is the breadth of the love of Christ*—Embracing all mankind, *and length*—From everlasting to everlasting, *and depth*—Not to be fathomed by any creature, *and height*—Not to be reached by any enemy. (ENNT)

The apostle wanted them to have this personal experience of the love of Christ so that they **may be filled to the measure of all the fullness of God** (Eph. 3:19). This is the climax of the entire prayer. But what did Paul mean? Surely we are not filled with the fullness of God in the same way Christ was (Col. 1:19; 2:9), though that might have been on Paul's mind since Ephesians and Colossians were written at the same time. The difficulty with this phrase exists only when we think in individual terms. It is the church that constitutes the fullness of God. In Ephesians 4:11–13, Paul talked about the use of spiritual gifts for the edification of the body of Christ "until we all reach unity in the faith and in the knowledge of the Son of God and become mature, attaining to the whole measure of the fullness of Christ" (v. 13). The fullness of God finds its expression in the church that is growing and maturing, a church where each individual is exercising his or her spiritual gift out of love for God and others. As we are obedient to His commands and fulfill what He has called us to do as a church, we enjoy a foretaste of what God has in store for us for eternity, when we will know His fullness in a much greater sense.

WORDS FROM WESLEY

Ephesians 3:19

And to know—But the apostle corrects himself, and immediately observes, it cannot be fully known. This only we know, that the love of *Christ* surpasses all knowledge, *that ye may be filled*—Which is the sum of all, *with all the fulness of God*—With all His light, love, wisdom, holiness, power, and glory. A perfection far beyond a bare freedom from sin. (ENNT)

Paul's Praise for the Father (Eph. 3:20-21)

Paul closed his prayer with a doxology. Much of what he had prayed seems impossible: to know the unknowable, to be united with the church triumphant, to be filled with the fullness of God. Perhaps his readers would have been discouraged at such lofty expectations. Paul acknowledged the greatness of God by declaring that He **is able to do immeasurably more than all we ask or imagine** (v. 20). What we feel weak and powerless to accomplish, God is more than adequate to do through us. Paul was confident that no matter what they asked or imagined, be it a vision for outreach ministry or individual maturity, God is limitless in His resources and is able to do even more. This He does **according to his power that is at work within us** (v. 20). This is the power mentioned in 3:16 that is the work of the indwelling Holy Spirit in the believer's (and the church's) life. His power energizes us to accomplish the goal. "For it is God who works in you to will and to act according to his good purpose" (Phil. 2:13).

Paul resounded with praise for such a magnificent God: **to him be glory in the church and in Christ Jesus throughout all generations, for ever and ever! Amen** (Eph. 3:21). God is to be glorified both in the church and in Christ. The linking of the two together is incredible, raising the church to an unbelievably high position.

WORDS FROM WESLEY

Ephesians 3:20

Now to him—This doxology is admirably adapted to strengthen our faith that we may not stagger at the great things the apostle had been praying for, as if they were too much for God to give, or for us to expect from him, *that is able*—Here is a most beautiful gradation. When He has given us exceeding, yea, abundant blessings, still we may ask for more. And He is able to do it. But we may think of more than we have asked. He is able to do this also. Yea, and above all this: above all we ask; above all we can think: nay, exceedingly, abundantly above all we can either ask or think. (ENNT)

Paul's words of praise constitute the climax of the entire letter, as chapters 4–6 reveal the practical expressions of all that is contained in the first three chapters. It is the knowledge of God working in and through us, the commitment to knowing and expressing His love, and the recognition of our responsibility as a church to bring glory to an almighty God that propels us and makes possible the practical out-working of our theology that comprise the second half of Ephesians.

DISCUSSION

Many programs exist to build up one's physical strength; energy drinks abound and supplements and vitamin pills line pharmacy shelves. Most people want to be physically strong and healthy. Discuss what provisions are available to make believers spiritually strong and energetic.

1. Who is able to strengthen believers to be at their best for God?

2. Evangelist Billy Sunday remarked, "If Christians were as weak physically as they are spiritually, they wouldn't be able to take a single step." Was he overly critical? What comparison would you make between Christians' spiritual strength and their physical strength?

3. How did Paul's spiritual strength manifest itself in the midst of trials?

4. What do you do to make a guest welcome in your house? What are you doing to make Christ feel at home in your heart?

5. How would you define Christ's love in terms of its width? Its length? Its height? Its depth?

6. Nothing is too hard for the Lord. He is able to do more than all we ask or imagine. Knowing this, what valid big request will you make to God? What might you imagine that God can do in your life or in the life of the church you attend?

7. Paul prayed big prayers for the Ephesian believers. What big prayers will you pray for your fellow Christians?

8. Paul wanted the Ephesians to be strong so God would be glorified. How can you glorify God this week by being strong in the Lord?

PRAYER

Lord, please strengthen us out of Your glorious riches with power through Your Spirit in our inner being. May we gratefully receive from Your hand more than we could ever ask or imagine.

3

UNITY IN PRACTICE

Ephesians 4:1-16

Christian unity makes us mature, strong, and effective.

For any sports team to achieve a winning season, it must have unity. Divisiveness can turn a team into its biggest opponent. But internal unity often propels a team into the playoffs and even a championship. Even players with only average talent can accomplish great things when they band together as one under the guidance of their coach.

This study recognizes that it takes effort for a body of believers to enjoy a spirit of unity, but God has provided all the essentials to make unity a reality. Expect to be challenged by this study to achieve and maintain unity in your local church.

COMMENTARY

The book of Ephesians was one of several letters written by Paul while he was in prison. Even though it is addressed "to the saints in Ephesus" (1:1), it is more likely written to churches in the region around Ephesus. Ephesians does not address any particular questions or situations there. Instead, it lays forth an understanding of the church and its place in God's great plan of salvation for the world. The first three chapters address such themes as the blessings of God in Christ, salvation by grace through faith, the unity of believers, and the immeasurable resources of God. Chapter 4 signals a shift in focus from the theological to the practical. Now the question becomes, in light of all God has done for us, how do we live worthy of the calling we have received?

Called to Unity (Eph. 4:1-6)

Paul began by identifying himself **as a prisoner for the Lord** (v. 1). In 3:1, he called himself "the prisoner of Christ Jesus for the sake of you Gentiles," and while he regarded himself as a slave to Christ in respect to his calling, he occasionally spent time in prison as a result of that calling. By appealing to his imprisonment, he was saying, in effect, "Take note of what I am telling you. I am putting my life on the line for it."

His first exhortation was to **live a life worthy of the calling you have received** (4:1). Paul said God has done great things for us: He has blessed us with every spiritual blessing in Christ, adopted us as His children, sealed us with His Holy Spirit, made us alive with Christ, and reconciled us to himself and each other. The word **worthy** means "to balance the scales." God has done His part in giving us all we need for holiness and maturity; now it is our responsibility to live up to it.

WORDS FROM WESLEY

Ephesians 4:1

What is it to "walk worthy of the vocation wherewith we are called?" It should always be remembered that the word *walk*, in the language of the apostle, is of a very extensive signification. It includes all our inward and outward motions; all our thoughts, and words, and actions. It takes in, not only everything we do, but everything we either speak or think. It is, therefore, no small thing "to walk," in this sense of the word, "worthy of the vocation wherewith we are called"; to think, speak, and act in every instance, in a manner worthy of our Christian calling. (WJW, vol. 6, 397–398)

To live a worthy life, Paul specified four graces necessary for good relationships in the Christian community. First, we are to **be completely humble** (v. 2). Pride is the spiritual root of all sin, but unlike the pagan notion of groveling servitude, Christian humility is the laying aside of one's rights for the sake of another. Christ himself set the example and said that whoever would be greatest in the kingdom must become the servant of all. Second, Paul exhorted the Ephesians to be **gentle** (v. 2). A gentle person is one who has every instinct and passion under complete control. Like humility, gentleness is a prime contributor to unity. Third, Paul said we are to **be patient** (v. 2). While this can mean the ability to endure hardship, more often in the New Testament it means the reluctance to avenge wrongs. Patience, or longsuffering, means "long tempered." It is the ability to endure discomfort without fighting back. Finally, Paul said Christians are to bear **with one another in love** (v. 2). Christians had to invent a new word to distinguish Christian love from all other kinds of love. They called it *agape*, meaning unconquerable benevolence.

WORDS FROM WESLEY

Ephesians 1:2

The "forbearing one another in love" seems to mean, not only the not resenting anything, and the not avenging yourselves; not only the not injuring, hurting, or grieving each other, either by word or deed; but also the bearing one another's burdens; yea, and lessening them by every means in our power. It implies the sympathizing with them in their sorrows, afflictions, and infirmities; the bearing them up when, without our help, they would be liable to sink under their burdens; the endeavouring to lift their sinking heads, and to strengthen their feeble knees. (WJW, vol. 6, 399)

By diligently exercising these graces, believers will be able to **keep the unity of the Spirit through the bond of peace** (v. 3). The absence of these graces jeopardizes unity. The verb here suggests unity will be difficult and will require resolute determination to accomplish. In fact, it can only be accomplished through the inner working of the Holy Spirit.

Paul went on to say there are seven reasons why the church must continually strive for unity. Among other things, **there is one body** (v. 4). The church of Jesus Christ is comprised of all believers of all nations who acknowledge Christ as Lord and are saved by grace through faith. Christ himself is the Head, and all the individual members have distinct functions, but together they form one body. And there is only **one Spirit** (v. 4). The same Holy Spirit who descended upon the church at Pentecost also filled the Gentiles gathered in Cornelius's house and the disciples of John in Ephesus. The one Holy Spirit unifies the church, placing each individual member into the body of Christ. In addition, believers are **called to one hope** (v. 4), namely, a world redeemed through Jesus Christ. No matter what happens in this life, Christians live with the common hope that Christ will one day return for His church and conquer the hosts of evil.

Believers must also strive for unity because they have **one Lord** (v. 5). As Lord, Jesus Christ is in charge. Disunity inevitably results whenever self-will supersedes the divine will. Unity should also result from the confession of **one faith** (v. 5). We are all saved by grace through faith. It is the common means of procuring our salvation. But faith is also the common core of Christian truth that was passed on from Christ to the apostles. Unity should also be a by-product of **one baptism** (v. 5). Even though the modes have differed between traditions, baptism has always been the universal declaration of faith among Christians of all ages. Finally, Paul declared there is **one God and Father of all** (v. 6). Unlike the pagans (both then and now), who have many gods, Christians have only one. And unlike the pagans, they are all children of one heavenly Father, brothers and sisters in relation to God and one another.

Equipped for Service (Eph. 4:7–13)

After talking about unity within the body of Christ, Paul moved the discussion to one of diversity and individuality. The whole body is made up of many parts, each with its own function and responsibility. **To each one**, Paul said, **grace has been given as Christ apportioned it** (v. 7). **Grace** here does not refer specifically to spiritual gifts themselves but to the fact that gifts come from the gracious hand of God. Everyone is endowed with certain natural abilities at birth, but in the "new birth" spiritual gifts are also apportioned to believers to enable them to fulfill spiritual ministry.

As a proof of this distribution of gifts by the Lord, Paul loosely quoted from Psalm 68:18, stating, **when he ascended on high, he led captives in his train and gave gifts to men** (Eph. 4:8). It was a picture of a conquering king entering a city with his captives in tow, throwing money to the cheering throngs. Paul interpreted the Psalm to say that when Christ sets believers free from their captivity to Satan, they become His servants and He in turn rewards them with special gifts.

Paul's discussion of spiritual gifts appears to become somewhat sidetracked in verses 9–10 as he digressed on the meaning of the word *ascended*. Ascension, he felt, had no meaning unless we understand that Jesus first came down from heaven. When He did this, His body was physically present on the earth, ministering to the hurts and needs of people. But when He ascended into heaven, He was no longer present on the earth. Nevertheless, He did make it possible for His "body" to fill the whole universe by equipping His church to do even greater things than He had done.

The list of spiritual gifts Paul mentioned here is very different than those listed in 1 Corinthians 12 and Romans 12. One reason could be that none of the lists is complete in itself, and perhaps not even complete when taken together. God has a diversity of gifts needed to fulfill the tasks He calls the church to complete. The gifts may very likely be different in each congregation. But another reason could be that the four he mentioned are not gifts at all, but gifted people God gives to the church to equip individual believers to do the works of ministry where their gifts will function.

First, Paul mentioned **apostles** (Eph. 4:11). Strictly speaking, an apostle was one who witnessed the life, death, and resurrection of Christ and was sent out by Him with a special commission to establish His church. It included the Twelve, but also Paul, Barnabas, James the brother of Jesus, Silvanus, Andronicus, and Junias (and perhaps others). In this sense, the role of apostle ceased when the last one died. However, in a more general sense, Christ still sends forth people today who know Him and have witnessed His power. The difference is that the foundation has been long established and any present-day "apostle" speaks only with the authority found in Scripture.

Second, Paul mentioned **prophets** (v. 11). A prophet was an itinerant minister who went from church to church with direct messages from God through the Holy Spirit. Prophets have never been received well in the church because it is difficult to discern the true gift from its false counterparts. And many question the need for the prophet today, since we now have the complete Word of God.

Third, Paul mentioned **evangelists** (v. 11). This "herald of the good news" was also a wanderer but was more likely to stay for longer periods in a given location than the apostle or prophet. Evangelists correspond today to what we call "missionaries." All believers have the responsibility to be witnesses for Christ, but some are especially called by God to do the work of an evangelist.

Finally, Paul spoke of **pastors and teachers** (v. 11). These two roles are complementary and are often coordinated in the same person. The word *pastor* means, quite literally, "shepherd." The pastor/teacher was entrusted with the nurture, protection, and supervision of the flock.

These four groups of people are gifts from Christ to the church **to prepare God's people for works of service** (v. 12). They are not the only ones entrusted with the work of ministry; all Christians are ministers. The function of these gifted leaders is to equip and enable the individual parts of the body to discover, coordinate, and use their God-given gifts in serving others. Then **the body of Christ** will **be built up** (v. 12). Individual Christians are built up when they are active in ministry, and the body of Christ is built up when gifts function in a healthy manner. And the end result of the church's engagement in active ministry is **unity in the faith** (v. 13) and maturity, becoming more like Christ in holiness and service.

WORDS FROM WESLEY
Ephesians 4:16

"Holy solitaries" is a phrase no more consistent with the gospel than holy adulterers. The gospel of Christ knows of no religion, but social; no holiness but social holiness. "Faith working by love" is the length and breadth and depth and height of Christian perfection. "This commandment have we from Christ, that he who loves God, love his brother also"; and that we manifest our love "by doing good unto all men; especially to them that are of the household of faith." And in truth, whosoever loveth his brethren, not in word only, but as Christ loved him, cannot but be "zealous of good works." He feels in his soul a burning, restless desire of spending and being spent for them. "My Father," will he say, "worketh hitherto, and I work." And at all possible opportunities he is, like his Master, "going about doing good." (WJW, vol. 14, 321–322)

Directed toward Maturity (Eph. 4:14–16)

God did not give new birth to believers intending that they remain as **infants** (v. 14). His goal is holiness and maturity (Eph. 1:4; 3:13). A church should never feel that it has succeeded by simply introducing people to the kingdom. God gave gifted people to the church to build it up in the faith and equip its members to do the works of ministry God had designed it to do (Eph. 2:10; 3:11–12). Baby Christians are unstable, **blown here and there by every wind of teaching** (4:14) that pops up in the world, and even at times in the church itself. But when the church is functioning in a healthy manner, when truth is being faithfully proclaimed in an environment of love, then the members will find themselves growing **up into him who is the Head, that is, Christ** (v. 15). The whole body—mysteriously joined together by a network of spiritual bones, muscles, and ligaments while receiving its direction from the Head—**builds itself up in love, as each part does its work** (v. 16).

DISCUSSION

A walk can be successful and enjoyable only when both feet move in unity as instructed by the brain. Similarly, God's people move forward in unity only as they obey the Head of the church.

1. How does *agape* love differ from the kind of love the entertainment industry often promotes?

2. What examples of *agape* love have you seen in your fellowship of believers?

3. How does unity contribute to spiritual maturity?

4. How would you answer the claim that it doesn't matter what Christians believe as long as they love one another?

5. Do you agree or disagree that a divisive church has a poor reputation in the community? Why?

6. Why does it demand "effort" to preserve the unity of the Spirit? How much effort have you expended recently to preserve this unity? What future effort will you expend?

7. Gossip often destroys a church's unity. What actions will you take to squelch gossip?

PRAYER

Father, forgive us for separating the body of Christ into our own kind and our own desires. Grant us the gift of unity and help us to add our differences to the one holy church.

4

REDEMPTIVE RELATIONSHIPS

Ephesians 5:22—6:9; Colossians 3:18—4:1

How we relate to others reveals how we relate to Christ.

Jesus told His followers to let their light shine before people so that they would see their good works and glorify our Father in heaven. We can let our light shine in the workplace and home as well as in our gatherings with fellow Christians. Darkness can never snuff out light, but hiding our light under a bushel will hinder our efforts to draw people from the darkness into the light of the gospel. This study will help us establish redemptive relationships as we shine for Jesus.

COMMENTARY

Although written to different audiences for different purposes, the similarities between Ephesians and Colossians are stunning, particularly in our study passages.

In Ephesians, Paul concentrated on the nature and witness of the church. He called his readers to unity in the faith and to "live a life worthy of the calling you have received" (4:1). Just before getting to the practical application of his message—how their new life in Christ was to affect their households (5:22—6:9)— Paul gave his readers the overarching principle that would ensure unity and a positive witness in the world: "Submit to one another out of reverence for Christ" (5:21). What Paul was suggesting is a spiritual principle that has ramifications for every area of social life. Mutual submission is based on the equality of believers in the body of Christ. Recognizing the equality of believers in

Christ would result in honor and submission to one another (doing what would benefit another). And such relationships within the church would naturally affect relationships in the home.

In Colossians 3, again the family relationship is described in the context of the believer's relationship with Christ. Again, recognizing our equality in Christ and being empowered by the Spirit lays the foundation for conduct in the Christian household. In Paul's day, women, children, and slaves had few rights. Slaves, an estimated sixty million of them comprising almost one-third of the total population of the Roman Empire, were considered mere property. From the time of Aristotle, codes of conduct had been developed by philosophers and moralists to dictate proper behavior in the home. Such codes were based on the absolute authority of the male head of the house and demanded absolute obedience from all the subordinates—wives, children, and slaves. Paul's treatment of the reciprocal nature of relationships in the home was revolutionary. While using the same standard form as the moralists, Paul said the head of the house had an obligation to treat subordinates in a manner consistent with Christianity.

Wives and Husbands (Eph. 5:22–33; Col. 3:18–19)

In both passages, the wife is urged to **submit** (Eph. 5:22; Col. 3:18) to her husband, and the husband is entreated to **love** (Eph. 5:25; Col. 3:19) his wife. This doesn't mean the husband has no obligation to submit to his wife, nor that the wife has no obligation to love her husband. Paul saw these two qualities, love and submission, as the foundation for good relationships in the home.

The word *submit* means to voluntarily give up one's own rights or will for the benefit of another. Wives are to submit to their husbands (in the context of mutual submission, Eph. 5:21) **as to the Lord** (v. 22) or **as is fitting in the Lord** (Col. 3:18). Her submission constitutes her service to the Lord and is befitting of a Christian wife. Notice, though, that Paul is not subjugating women to the dictates of men. His concern is with order and harmony in the home. **For the husband is the head of the wife as Christ is the head of the church, his body** (Eph. 5:23). As a member of the Trinity, Christ submitted himself to the will of God, though He was coequal and co-eternal with the Father. He didn't consider equality with God something to be forcefully retained, but in humility He gave up all He had to come to earth to serve (see Phil. 2:6–7). His position in the Godhead in no way diminished His deity or authority. So it is with the husband-wife relationship. Though the wife voluntarily submits to her husband, her submission is not a sign of weakness, subserviences, or inferiority. It is worth noting that Christ's headship over the church resulted in servanthood. Ultimately, being the Head meant He was willing to lay down His life for the church. In the home, the husband has been given the responsibility in the Lord for the protection and care of the family, and it is only natural that his wife would submit to his loving servant leadership since he has her best interests at heart. A Christian relationship is assumed here, making it possible for the wife to submit to her husband **in everything** (Eph. 5:24).

WORDS FROM WESLEY

Ephesians 5:25

Then am I bound (if charity
Divine be made the rule for me)
As my own flesh to love my wife,
And gladly ransom with my life
Her soul from the infernal grave;
For Jesus died, His church to save. (PW, vol. 13, 76)

Husbands are called to **love** their **wives, just as Christ loved the church and gave himself up for her** (v. 25). Paul used the verb *agapao* for love. It was not a romantic, erotic, or familial love he called the husband to, but the self-sacrificing love of Christ. Paul described the love Christ has for the church: He **gave himself up for her to make her holy . . . and to present her to himself as a radiant church . . . holy and blameless** (vv. 26–27). Far from seeking to control the church or to force her to submit to His authority, Christ's love undergirds the church and empowers it to become what He created it to be—holy and blameless in His sight. That's how husbands should love their wives. They lift up and help their wives become all God created them to be. This is not an issue of control or who's in charge. It's an issue of love and mutual submission in Christ.

Husbands, Paul went on to say, should **love their wives as their own bodies** (v. 28). Since Genesis 2:24 teaches that **the two will become one flesh** (Eph. 5:31), the husband is in fact acting in his own best interest when **he feeds and cares for** (literally, "nourishes and cherishes," v. 29) his wife. The two are inseparable. The unity of the marriage relationship is akin to Christ's unity with the church, His body.

WORDS FROM WESLEY

Ephesians 5:26

That he might sanctify it through the word—The ordinary channel of all blessings, *having cleansed it*—From the guilt and power of sin, *by the washing of water*—In baptism, if with the "outward and visible sign," we receive the inward and spiritual grace. (ENNT)

Although Paul used imagery here of a bride and bridegroom (for example, the **washing with water** in 5:26 alludes to the bride's prenuptial washing), he made it clear that he was **talking about Christ and the church** (v. 32). We must look to Christ's relationship with the church to guide us in our understanding of the marriage relationship, not the other way around.

WORDS FROM WESLEY
Ephesians 5:28

As their own bodies—That is, as themselves. *He that loveth his wife, loveth himself*—Which is not a sin, but an indisputable duty. (ENNT)

Paul summed up his teaching in Ephesians 5:33: **However, each one of you also must love his wife as he loves himself; and the wife must respect her husband.** Honor is at the heart of Paul's teaching for wives, not subservience.

Children and Fathers (Eph. 6:1–4; Col. 3:20–21)

All ancient moralists, including Jews, required obedience of children still living in their parents' homes, and grown children were expected to honor their parents. Paul upheld such expectations. Notice that Paul addressed children. They were part of the church and were expected to act in accordance with their newfound faith, **for this is right**. They were to **obey** their **parents in the Lord** (Eph. 6:1). Colossians 3:20 adds **for this pleases the Lord**. He made it clear that such obedience is part of the code of conduct for the Christian, no matter the age. It's part of the mutual submission and honor in all relationships that Paul had been advocating. Ephesians 6:2 adds the concept of honor by appealing to the fifth commandment (Ex. 20:12; Deut. 5:16). He said this **is the first commandment with a promise** (Eph. 6:2), **first** meaning it is the commandment of primary importance or significance for children, since in the Decalogue it is actually the second commandment with a promise (see Deut. 20:6). The promise for children who obey their parents as minors and continue to bring honor to them when grown is **that it may go well with you and that you may enjoy long life on the**

earth (Eph. 6:3). Children who learn the discipline and maturity associated with Christian submission and honor will certainly experience the goodwill of others in addition to their parents and will have learned the secret of success in all relationships.

Next Paul addressed **fathers** (heads of the household; Eph. 6:4), explaining that the relationship was to be reciprocal. (Note that the word used here for fathers, *pateron*, can also refer to parents, as in Heb. 11:23. The admonitions here also apply to mothers.) The moralists taught that fathers had a responsibility to force their children to obey. But Paul entreated them not to **embitter** (irritate or provoke) their children or cause them to **become discouraged** (Col. 3:21). Excessive discipline (or harshness) can kill the tender spirit of a child. The concept of mutual submission and love forces Christian parents to consider their children as fellow Christians and to nurture and cherish them. Instead of exasperating their children, parents should seek to **bring them up in the training and instruction of the Lord** (Eph. 6:4). The goal of discipline in the home is to train children to be holy, not just to enforce unquestioning obedience. Paul's teaching here is unprecedented. Is it any wonder that the status of both women and children has risen markedly in societies where Christianity has been preached?

Slaves and Masters (Eph. 6:5–9; Col. 3:22—4:1)

Slavery was an integral part of Greco-Roman society. While many slaves performed menial household duties or were craftsmen, the majority of teachers, doctors, and other "professionals" were also slaves. While Paul didn't call for the abolition of slavery, he certainly paved the way for it.

Paul cautioned slaves to live out their Christianity by submitting to their masters: **obey your earthly masters in everything** (Col. 3:22). Notice the repetition of **the Lord** in Colossians (vv. 22–24). Slaves needed to change their perspective. They were working for the Lord and should render service as unto Him. That means they would **serve wholeheartedly** (Eph. 6:7) and would **obey . . . with respect and fear, and with sincerity of heart** (v. 5). Instead of merely trying to **win their favor** (v. 6; Col. 3:22), slaves should instead seek to be God-pleasers (see 1 Thess. 2:4–6; Gal. 1:10). By reminding slaves that **the Lord will reward everyone for whatever good he does, whether he is slave or free** (Eph. 6:8) and **anyone who does wrong will be repaid for his wrong** (Col. 3:25), Paul communicated that slaves were on equal footing with their masters. Paul reminded slaves in Colossians 3:25 and masters in Ephesians 6:9 that **there is no favoritism**.

Like husbands and fathers, masters also have a responsibility to submit to their fellow Christians, both slave and free. In practical terms, it amounted to not threatening them (Eph. 6:9) and providing them **with what is right and fair** (Col. 4:1). Paul reminded them that they also had a heavenly Master (v. 1; Eph. 6:9). Christian masters should remember the Golden Rule and treat their slaves as they would want to be treated by their Master, Jesus Christ.

Slavery is not accepted in our society—in fact, its abolition in Western civilization largely came about due to the influence of the Christian gospel. The principles Paul taught here still apply to Christian employers and employees. We should honor one another above ourselves (Rom. 12:10) and "submit to one another out of reverence for Christ" (Eph. 5:21). Our Christianity should influence our day-to-day walk in the world.

DISCUSSION

Interpersonal relationships may be splintered rather than splendid. A marriage may end in divorce. A congregation may split. Christians may sever friendships over personal preferences.

1. What interpersonal relations does the apostle Paul discuss in the study Scripture?

2. Where do you think it is hardest to maintain godly relationships: home, workplace, school, or church? Why?

3. What do you see as the greatest threats to marriage today? How might a Christian couple withstand these threats?

4. Do you think it is harder to lead a godly life as an employer or as an employee? Why?

5. What do you think would happen in the workplace if an employer and employees put Paul's counsel into practice?

6. Husbands are commanded to love their wives "as Christ loved the church and gave himself up for her." What are some practical ways a husband can show this kind of love to his wife?

7. Wives are not commanded to love their husbands. Why do you think this command is not given?

PRAYER

Our God, who has provided us with a blessed relationship of love and grace, please help us relate to the people You have given us with the same forgiving, loving, and affirming action, "doing the will of God" from our hearts.

5

HOW TO BE STRONG IN THE LORD

Ephesians 6:10–24

Our strength is in the full armor of God.

Nations that fight to defeat tyranny and terrorism provide their military forces with the best possible weapons and body armor. But what disaster would occur if our military rejected those provisions and chose instead to go into battle unarmed and wearing jeans, T-shirts, and sneakers?

The Devil and his forces employ diabolical tactics and deadly weapons in their war against us. We must not engage this sinister enemy in our own strength, but avail ourselves of the weapons God has given. We must put on the whole armor of God and be strong in the Lord.

This study will challenge you to "be strong in the Lord and in his mighty power" (Eph. 6:10).

COMMENTARY

Paul had been instructing the Ephesians in practical, Christian living. They were to put off the old self and put on the new (4:20–24). This new life is characterized by integrity, generosity, wholesome speech, a forgiving attitude (4:25–32), sexual purity (5:3–5), and joyful sobriety (5:15–19). And it includes proper daily relationships (5:21–33; 6:1–4, 5–9). But how can we live this life? Earlier in this letter, Paul talked about the mighty power of God available for us—the power that raised Jesus from the dead and exalted Him to the Father's right far above every other power (1:19–23). It is only through this power that we will be able to live the wonderful Christian life Paul described for us. In the final verses of this letter, he challenged us to take the resources God has provided and use them.

Be Prepared (Eph. 6:10–13)

Be strong (v. 10) is better understood as "be strengthened." We must draw our strength from the Lord by trusting in Him, waiting on Him in prayer, and obeying Him. We are weak, but the Lord's mighty power is available to us. Living the Christian life is like a battle for which we must **put on the full armor of God** (v. 11). This is Paul's description of the resources God has for us. It includes everything both defensive and offensive we need to live the Christian life and fight the Christian fight. If we draw on these resources, we will be able to successfully **take** our **stand against the devil's schemes** (v. 11). The Devil has many deceitful ways of entrapping us. Only with God's armor can we escape him.

WORDS FROM WESLEY

Ephesians 6:10

Be strong—Nothing less will suffice for such a fight. To be weak, and remain so, is the way to perish: *in the power of his might*—A very uncommon expression: plainly denoting what great assistance we need. As if His might would not do: it must be the powerful exertion of His might. (ENNT)

In any fight, part of being prepared is knowing your enemy. It is not profitable to become preoccupied with one's enemy, but it is wise to know what one is up against. Paul told us clearly, **our struggle is not against flesh and blood** (v. 12). Our enemies are not human, and therefore we are no match for them! They are supernatural, demonic. It is not possible to distinguish clearly between **rulers, authorities,** and **powers** (v. 12). These are spiritual beings who oppose us and God. They promote the values of the evil world around us, attempt to control the world in which we live, and make it **dark** by trying to exclude the light of God's truth. They are indeed **spiritual forces of evil**, and the battle is not a human struggle but a battle **in the heavenly realms** (v. 12), in the spiritual dimension. But God has already blessed us in this same spiritual dimension with Christ (1:3). The exalted Christ has already won the victory over all of these spiritual forces, as well as all temporal forces (1:10–21), and uses this power for us, His church (1:22–23). These evil forces have been defeated in principle, but the time is still future when God will put this victory into full effect and all will be visibly united under the rule of Christ (1:10). In the meantime, we must draw on Christ's strength to overcome these spiritual forces.

If we **put on the full armor of God**, we will be able to be victorious in **the day of evil** (6:13). In one sense, every day is a day of evil. We live in the time of temptation, the time in which we are exposed to **the devil's schemes** (v. 11). There are, however, particular times when the Enemy seems to assault us with determined strength. It will seem like we have to do **everything** possible to successfully resist and **stand** our **ground** (v. 13). First Corinthians 10:13 assures us that God will never let us be tempted above what we are able. His armor will always be sufficient for us.

Put on Your Armor (Eph. 6:14–17)

Paul described the resources God has for us as the various pieces of a soldier's equipment. He may have written this letter from his Roman prison with a soldier standing by him. Perhaps he looked at the various pieces of armor as he wrote. How important for people to put on **the belt of truth** (v. 14). People in Paul's world wore long flowing robes. If they were going to run, work hard, or fight, they gathered up this robe and tucked it securely under a belt. Then they were prepared for activity. **Truth** prepares us to fight the good fight. Of course the true message of the gospel of Jesus Christ is essential. But Paul was probably also referring to our integrity. By God's power, we must maintain integrity in all we do. How important the **breastplate of righteousness** is (v. 14). The breastplate protected all the vital organs—heart, lungs, stomach, liver, kidneys. Right conduct empowered by God is vital protection. As long as we live in obedience to God, we are protected from mortal wound. Disobedience makes us vulnerable.

The mobility of a soldier is crucial. The soldier's feet must be **fitted** (v. 15) with shoes that give him a **readiness** to share the good news of the **gospel**. Sharing the gospel with others is essential to the victorious Christian life. How surprising that in the midst of this battle imagery the gospel is called the **gospel of peace** (v. 15). But the object of war is restored peace. Usually wars do not accomplish this purpose. The "war to end all wars" (World War I) did not bring permanent peace. But the gospel does bring peace; it brings a wholeness of restored relationships with God, others, and the world.

The **shield of faith** (v. 16) is an absolute necessity. Paul was thinking of the large Roman shield. It was about four feet high and maybe two-and-a-half feet wide. This shield was designed to cover the whole body. Absolute trust in our Lord stops the arrows of temptation and trial the Enemy may shoot at us. **Flaming arrows** were particularly dangerous. They could pierce and set the soldiers' clothes, tent, or supplies on fire. The shield of faith stops the worst the Enemy can do. If we doubt God or focus on the Enemy instead of on Christ, we allow these arrows to smolder and burn. Faith covers and protects all the other armor.

Over all is the **helmet of salvation** (v. 17). We have been saved from the guilt and power of sin. Sin need no longer control us. We have the assured hope of eternal salvation (1:18). We can face the Enemy because God through Christ has delivered us from our past and assured our future.

Finally we come to the great offensive weapon: **the sword** that **the Spirit** gives us (6:17). The Spirit also directs and empowers us in the use of this sword. What is this great sword? The powerful creative **word of God** that brought the worlds into existence, revealed His truth to the prophets, became incarnate in Christ (John 1:1, 14), penetrates to the depths of the human person (Heb. 4:12–13), and recreates us anew in Christlikeness (Rom. 10:17; Eph. 1:13; Col. 3:16; 1 Thess. 2:13; 2 Thess. 3:1). As we hear, read, and study this Word as we have it in the Bible, the Holy Spirit makes it alive, which renews us, defeats the Enemy, and liberates others. Jesus gives us a matchless example of using the Word of God to overcome temptation in Matthew 4:1–11. Notice how our shield and sword work together. It is faith that allows His Word to be effective in our lives.

WORDS FROM WESLEY

Ephesians 6:17

And take for an helmet the hope *of salvation*—(1 Thess. 5:8). The head is that part which is most carefully to be defended. One stroke here may prove fatal. The armour, for this is the hope of salvation. The lowest degree of this hope is a confidence that God will work the whole work of faith in us: the highest is a full assurance of future glory, added to the experimental knowledge of pardoning love. Armed with this helmet (the hope of the joy set before Him). Christ endured the cross and despised the shame. Hebrews 12:2 and the sword of the Spirit, *the word of God*—This Satan cannot withstand, when it is edged and wielded by faith. Till now our armour has been only defensive. But we are to attack Satan, as well as secure ourselves: the shield in one hand, and the sword in the other. Whoever fights with the powers of hell will need both. He that is covered with armour from head to foot, and neglects this, will be foiled after all. This whole description shows us how great a thing it is to be a Christian. The want of any one thing makes him incomplete. (ENNT)

Be Alert (Eph. 6:18–20)

Soldiers must not sleep or be distracted when on duty. Christian soldiers are alert when they continually **pray in the Spirit** (v. 18). Just as the Christian's use of God's Word is empowered and directed by the Spirit, so prayer is empowered and directed by the Spirit. The Spirit enables us to both listen to God's Word and talk to Him. In prayer, the Christian soldier receives his orders and intelligence reports of the Enemy. He is directed far more effectively than he could ever direct himself. Thus, it is important to always pray in every situation and **with all kinds of prayers and requests**, bringing every need to the Commander! His sufficiency, knowledge of the Enemy, and direction are supreme.

WORDS FROM WESLEY
Ephesians 6:18

Though he has his loins girt with truth, righteousness for a breast-plate, his feet shed with the preparation of the gospel, the shield of faith, the helmet of salvation, and the sword of the Spirit: yet one thing he wants after all, What is that? It follows,

Praying always—At all times, and on every occasion, in the midst of all employments, inwardly praying without ceasing; *by the Spirit*—Through the influence of the Holy Spirit, *with all prayer*—With all sort of prayer, public, private, mental, vocal . . . *and supplication*—Repeating and urging our prayer, as Christ did in the garden, *and watching*—Inwardly attend upon God to know His will, to gain power to do it, and to attain to the blessings we desire, *with all perseverance*—Continuing to the end in this holy exercise, *and supplication for all the saints*—Wrestling in fervent, continued intercession for others, especially for the faithful, that they may do all the will of God, and be steadfast to the end. Perhaps we receive few answers to prayer, because we do not intercede enough for others. (ENNT)

We do not fight alone. We are part of an army. The Roman soldier fought as part of an organized and well-disciplined team.

If we are truly **alert** soldiers, we keep on **praying for all the saints** (v. 18). When we don't hold others up in prayer, we are like a soldier asleep at his post.

Paul also needed their prayers. Although he was a prisoner in Rome, he did not ask for prayer for his safety. He did not ask for prayer that he be freed. It is, of course, quite right to pray for these things. But Paul's chief concern was the right words to be given him so that he could effectively preach the gospel (v. 19). That was his first concern. Then he asked for what every good soldier needs—boldness. **That I will fearlessly make known the mystery of the gospel** (v. 19). Being a soldier of Christ is not just overcoming temptation; it is actively proclaiming God's Word, calling others to Christ, and opposing evil in all its forms!

WORDS FROM WESLEY

Ephesians 6:20

An ambassador in bonds—The ambassadors of men usually appear in great pomp. How differently does the ambassador of Christ appear? (ENNT)

This was not the first time Paul called himself an **ambassador** (v. 20) for Christ (see 2 Cor. 5:20). He was the special representative of the heavenly King to this world. In our present verse, he was God's special representative to Rome. Paul was an ambassador **in chains** (Eph. 6:20). But again, it was not freedom that was foremost in his mind. He asked for prayer that he would fearlessly fulfill his ambassadorial mission. His great desire was to faithfully proclaim God's Word (see Acts 4:29; 5:40–42). May God help us to be more concerned about proclaiming His Word and doing His will than about the immediate consequences to ourselves.

God's Grace Be with You (Eph. 6:21–24)

Tychicus (v. 21) was a Gentile companion of Paul from the Roman province of Asia (Acts 20:4). It is not surprising that Paul would entrust him on this occasion to carry letters to Ephesus and Colosse (Col. 4:7–8), cities in his home province. He also appeared as a messenger of Paul in 2 Timothy 4:12 and Titus 3:12. Paul's affection was expressed in the term **dear brother** (Eph. 6:21). Tychicus was **faithful** in his service to the Lord. Thus, Paul had much confidence in him. No doubt the Christians in Ephesus and in the rest of the province of Asia were anxious to hear news of their beloved Paul from Tychicus. Tychicus himself would **encourage** (v. 22) them in their Christian walk. Such encouragement should always be the aim of Christian fellowship.

Paul closed his letter by wishing the very best for his readers. **Peace** (v. 23) is wholeness of relationships with God and others, well-being. Christlike **love** is to be characteristic of Christian conduct and is closely associated with this wholeness. Both come from **faith**, true commitment to Jesus Christ. It is God who gives this peace, love, and faith through the work of the Lord Jesus Christ. God's **grace** (v. 24), His own goodness, is the source of all these blessings. Paul wished an abundance of this grace for all true Christians, those who truly and sincerely **love our Lord Jesus Christ** (v. 24). By means of this grace they would be able to stand firm in their Christian lives.

DISCUSSION

Discuss what elements of the armor of God most appeal to you and what each represents.

1. How powerful is Satan? Is he omnipotent? On what do you base your answers? How seriously do you take him? Why?

2. In spiritual warfare, do you believe the Christian's posture should be defensive, offensive, or both? Explain.

3. Why do you agree or disagree that satanic schemes are being implemented in modern politics, education, and secular entertainment?

4. How does Satan attack the mind? The heart?

5. Do you think it is as hard to stand in victory as it is to stand in battle? Why or why not?

6. What does it mean to pray in the Spirit?

7. Soldiers employ the buddy system as a security measure. What evidence of the buddy system do you see in these verses?

8. What specific personal prayer request did Paul give the Ephesians?

9. How might you serve as a more effective ambassador for Christ?

PRAYER

Lord, give us the skills and weapons necessary to engage the Enemy. Help us to stand firm and not retreat, but be fearless to declare Your Word.

6

VICTORIOUS CHRISTIAN LIVING IN TOUGH TIMES

Philippians 1:1–30

God gives us whom we need to stand firm.

Blest be the tie that binds." John Fawcett penned these words after his congregation gathered around the wagon that held his household goods. He was ready to move from the little country church where he served as pastor to a big city church. However, when he looked into the tear-filled eyes of his congregation, he unloaded the wagon and stayed at the little church the rest of his life.

Paul and the Philippian believers enjoyed a tight bond of fellowship that promoted victorious Christian living. Neither Paul nor the Philippians were self-centered; they truly cared about each other. This study will help you live victoriously by building a loving relationship with the Lord and one another.

COMMENTARY

Paul wrote this letter to the Philippians when he was in prison in Rome. In those days, prisons were used to hold people for trial, and, unless a prisoner had friends on the outside, he had no one to take care of him. So Epaphroditus came from Philippi to care for Paul's needs while he was in prison. He brought a letter to Paul from the Philippian Christians and told him how things were going. Paul wrote this letter back to the church and sent it with Epaphroditus. Paul prayed his letter would help their "love abound more and more in knowledge and depth of insight, so that [they would] be able to discern what is best and may be pure and blameless until the day of Christ" (Phil. 1:9–10).

Paul loved the Philippians, and they loved him. Their love produced a "fellowship in the gospel," which today we might call a sense of community. Acts 16 tells the story of how the Philippian church began. Lydia and some other women had gathered outside Philippi to pray. Paul and his companions went to talk to them. "The Lord opened her heart to respond to Paul's message . . . [and] she and the members of her household were baptized" (16:14–15). After that, Lydia invited them to her home, saying, "If you consider me a believer in the Lord . . . come and stay at my house" (16:15). Lydia understood that fellowship was at the heart of her new faith. By becoming an intimate part of the community of believers, we show others how much we believe in Jesus. The more we believe, the more we will be a part of the community of faith.

Servants, Saints, Overseers, and Deacons (Phil. 1:1)

In the ancient world, the beginning of a letter was quite important. This is definitely true with Philippians. The first verse sets the tone for the entire letter, but there are questions to be answered. Why did Paul call himself a servant when he usually called himself an apostle? Who are the **saints**? What are the jobs of the **overseers** and **deacons** (v. 1)? What is the difference between them? To answer these questions, we must look at how the words relate to each other. Is it important that they were written in this order: servants, saints, overseers, and deacons? What would that tell us about the Christians of Philippi? Most importantly, how will that help us learn more from God's Word? How can we become more mature Christians by answering these questions?

Paul had his own style of writing. He liked to start out writing about one thing, then move on to other things, and then return to his original topic. When he did this, Paul was trying to show the relationship between things, sometimes things that seem unrelated. He did this in verse 1. He wanted to show the relationship between **servants**, **saints**, **overseers**, and **deacons**. So, some-how, **servants** and **overseers and deacons** have similar mean-ings, because they form brackets around **saints**.

Paul's style echoed the teachings of Jesus, even though he did not usually quote Christ. It is possible that Jesus' teaching in Matthew 20:25–27 (and the parallel in Mark 10:42–44) underlies Paul's use of the word *servant* in Philippians 1:1. In these verses, the word translated as "servant" is the same word translated as **deacon** in Philippians 1:1. Also, the word translated as "slave" is the same word translated as "servant" in Philippians. What does this mean? It means that "deacon" is a more specific word for "servant."

So Paul was reminding the Philippians that Christian leadership is in direct opposition to Gentile (Roman or otherwise) leadership. Paul called himself and Timothy a servant-slave of Christ Jesus, which he understood in the context of being a servant-slave to all the saints who are in Christ Jesus. If Paul served Jesus, who is the Head of the church and the greatest servant of the church (Matt. 20:28), then Paul also served the whole church. No one would deny that Paul was a leader and authority figure in the early church and even today. However, he understood that his authority and leadership came from his service to Jesus and the church.

What about overseer? What is the relationship between over-seer and deacon? The best place to look for help with this is Acts 6, where the disciples chose seven from among their number to be deacons or servants of the daily rations given to the widows. An argument arose about fairness between the Hebrew and Greek widows. The leading apostles decided they needed time to be the servant-deacons of the Word and prayer. So they elected seven men "known to be full of the Spirit and wisdom," and they handed the service to the widows over to them. The authority over that ministry was given to those men, along with the responsibility of the ministry. Thus, it seems that **overseers and deacons**

(Phil. 1:1) should be read as separate but equal aspects of the ministry in Philippi. It also suggests a specific designation for those who would enter full-time participation in ministry.

By placing **saints** between **servants** and **overseers and deacons**, Paul emphasized again the communal nature of Christianity. Our concern as Christians is not for ourselves or our positions, but for the body of Christ, that the whole church might be edified and strengthened because of our service. In the final judgment, there will be two categories: saints and sinners. The church is a living representation of the final judgment. The highest title we can attain is that of "saint in Christ Jesus," which Jesus himself confers on us through our faith.

Verse 1 serves to establish the identity of everyone in regard to their relationship to Jesus and others. This is quite a loud echo of the Great Commandment. It is the establishment of a community.

The Fellowship of Grace (Phil. 1:2–11)

Paul thanked God for the Philippians and prayed with joy for them **because of** their **partnership in the gospel from the first day until now** (v. 5). The word **partnership** can be translated "fellowship." It is the same word we find in Acts 2:42: "They devoted themselves to the apostles' teaching and to the fellowship." What is this fellowship? What does it mean to be partners in the gospel? It means at least four things. First, it is being confident that God will finish the work He has begun in all believers (Phil. 1:6). Sometimes we can be discouraged at the lack of spiritual growth in others, especially those we are discipling ourselves. We must remember that God began the spiritual work, and He will finish it. Our job is to encourage and rebuke gently and in love. Second, having a partner in the gospel means having someone in your heart no matter where you are or what the circumstances (v. 7). The fellowship of grace binds believers so close that no degree of separation can break the bond between them. Third, partners in the gospel long to be with each other **with the affection of Christ** (v. 8). This means we have a sacrificial love for one another. We will sacrifice money, time, and comfort for the chance to personally help another believer. Finally, a partnership in the gospel means that we build up one another in our faith (vv. 9–11). We pray for the spiritual growth of others so that **the glory and praise of God** (v. 11) might fill the whole earth.

WORDS FROM WESLEY
Philippians 1:7

Partakers of my grace—That is, sharers in the afflictions, which God vouchsafed me as a grace or favour (ver. 29, 30), both in my bonds, and when I was called forth to answer for myself, and to confirm the gospel. It is not improbable, that after they had endured that great trial of affliction, God had sealed them [referring back to 1:6] unto full victory, of which the apostle had a prophetic sight. (ENNT)

Manner Worthy of the Gospel (Phil. 1:12–30)

Verse 27 conveys Paul's main point. Regardless of future events, the Philippians must act in a manner that reflects the gospel. How were they to do that? By standing **firm in one spirit, contending as one man for the faith of the gospel without being frightened in any way by those who oppose** them (vv. 27–28). In other words, they were to remain unified, committed to the community of faith, no matter what happened. Let's look back at the beginning of this section and see how this theme is displayed.

In verse 12, Paul said his imprisonment **has really served to advance the gospel**. He said everyone knew he was in jail because he preached Christ (v. 13); but, more interestingly, his chains encouraged **most of the brothers in the Lord . . . to speak the word of God more courageously and fearlessly** (v. 14). If we will remain unified in times of trouble, we will see

God's hand at work. We will understand how God can bring good out of bad. If God raised Jesus from the dead, He brought the ultimate good (life) out of the ultimate bad (death). Therefore, we must remain faithful to the fellowship. That is living a life worthy of the gospel of Christ.

WORDS FROM WESLEY
Philippians 1:11

Being filled with the fruits of righteousness, which are through Jesus Christ, to the glory and praise of God—Here are three properties of that sincerity which is acceptable to God. 1. It must bear fruits, the fruits of righteousness, all inward and outward holiness, all good tempers, words, and works, and that so abundantly, that we may be filled with them; 2. The branch and the fruits must derive both their virtue and their very being from the all-supporting, all-supplying root, Jesus Christ; 3. As all these flow from the grace of Christ, so they must issue in the glory and praise of God. (ENNT)

What happens to those who live for themselves in the guise of living for Christ, those with no heart for the community, only selfish ambition? Paul said it made no difference. If Christ is preached, Christ will be believed. If Christ is believed, God will finish the work. God's power is greater than any heresy or selfish ambition. The difference is that those who are not dedicated to maintaining unity within the church will find themselves outside the fellowship of grace with no partnership in the gospel.

So what do we have left to do but rejoice? If we have the prayers of others and the help of the Spirit of Jesus, everything that happens to us has the potential to bring glory to God. There is nothing for us to fear. Paul said he knew he would **in no way be ashamed** (v. 20). The basic meaning of being ashamed is fear—fear that we put our trust in the wrong place, fear that our faith will turn out to be insufficient, fear that our beliefs will be shown to be false. The opposite is courage—courage to speak of the goodness of God in times of suffering, especially if that suffering is because of our belief in God. It is only when we suffer together that we truly commune together. Many are willing to rejoice together, but far fewer are willing to suffer together. However, true rejoicing brings a willingness to suffer, and suffering brings an authenticity to rejoicing. Therefore Christians rejoice together and suffer together. We love, laugh, cry, mourn, call out to God, pray for His comfort and guidance, pray for the salvation of others—together in a manner worthy of the gospel of Christ.

WORDS FROM WESLEY
Philippians 1:29

Consider the words of St. Paul: 'To you it is given, in the behalf of Christ'—for his sake, as a fruit of his death and intercession for you—'not only to believe, but also to suffer for his sake' (Phil. 1:29). *It is given!* God gives you this opposition or reproach; it is a fresh token of His love. And will you disown the Giver; or spurn His gift, and count it a misfortune? Will you not rather say, 'Father, the hour is come, that thou shouldest be glorified: Now thou givest thy child to suffer something for thee: Do with me according to thy will?' Know that these things, far from being hinderances to the work of God, or to your soul, unless by your own fault, are not only unavoidable in the course of Providence, but profitable, yea, necessary, for you. Therefore, receive them from God (not from chance) with willingness, with thankfulness. (WJW, vol. 11, 434)

DISCUSSION

Everyone has trouble at one time or another, but victory over trouble is available.

1. How would you describe the tough conditions under which Paul wrote the letter to the Philippians?

2. You have heard it said, "I am doing all right *under* the circumstances." Why do you agree or disagree that it is possible to live *above* the circumstances?

3. What made the Philippian Christians so special to Paul? Why are your fellow Christians special to you?

4. What good work is God accomplishing in your life? How might you cooperate with Him in this work?

5. Why must love and knowledge achieve a perfect balance?

6. Paul recognized God's hand in his incarceration. How do you see God's hand working in a difficult situation that you are facing?

7. How have the prayers of fellow believers helped you maintain a positive attitude in past adversity? How earnestly do you pray for fellow Christians who are undergoing difficult trials?

8. What is most appealing to you about staying alive?

9. What is most appealing to you about heaven?

10. How can you use your experience with adversity to encourage a fellow believer?

PRAYER

O Lord, no matter what befalls us, good or bad, may the gospel of Jesus Christ be proclaimed and advanced.

7

HUMBLE LIKE GOD

Philippians 2:1-11

There is no place for a proud disciple in the service of a humble Master.

I'm just glad I had an opportunity to showcase my skills." The football player who mouthed these post-game-interview words had scored a couple of touchdowns, but we wouldn't give him any points for humility, would we? A humble player would most likely attribute the touchdowns to a total team effort.

More than a few Bible characters learned the hard way that God opposes the proud but gives grace to the humble. Pride reflects Satan's character, but humility reflects the character of Jesus. Humility also strengthens any body of believers. This study focuses on the humility Jesus showed by condescending to become a man and die for us. Expect to be challenged by this study to develop a greater degree of humility.

COMMENTARY

Some might say the entire context of Paul's letter to the Philippians is encouragement. This is certainly true of the first eleven verses of chapter 2. The immediate context of this section is set by the last two verses of chapter 1: "For it has been granted to you on behalf of Christ not only to believe on him, but also to suffer for him, since you are going through the same struggle you saw I had, and now hear that I still have" (vv. 29–30). Paul knew the Philippian church was under pressure from within its culture because of this new religion. In fact, Paul himself was accused in Philippi of "advocating customs unlawful for us

Romans to accept or practice" (Acts 16:21). As a result, Paul and Silas were beaten publicly and imprisoned.

Evidently, not much had changed since Paul left Philippi. His comment that they were going through the same struggle suggests that other Philippian Christians were beaten and in jail for the same reason. The governing officials of Philippi were trying to rid the city of a non-Roman religion. Philippi was proud of its Roman citizenship and considered itself a microcosm of Rome. Therefore, the traditional Roman religion was the only legal religion in the city, and the Philippian Christians were under extreme pressure to choose between their citizenship and their faith. This commentary is not able to explain the importance of citizenship in the ancient world, but let it suffice to say that having to choose between citizenship and anything else was equal to choosing between life and death, not only your own, but also your family's. The Philippians needed encouragement of the highest order. Paul intended to do just that by explaining their suffering in terms of a gift from God and fellowship with Christ, and by explaining how the incarnation of Christ established a pattern of righteous suffering that leads to eternal victory through obedience and death.

Use Your Faith—It Will Work (Phil. 2:1)

Verse 1 is Paul's dramatic way of telling the Philippians to focus on their faith and not on their circumstances. This concept underlies everything that follows in the next ten verses. The Greek sentence is written in such a way that the Philippians knew Paul was not questioning their commitment to Christianity, but confirming it. Paul told the Philippians not to worry, because in Christ they have the tools and abilities to survive their hardships. This is also the message we need to take from verse 1. We too should focus on our faith, not our circumstances, and then we will see how Christianity equips us to have victory over our trials and tribulations. The Lord knows we can overcome because He knows He will enable us to do just that.

The question is not our ability to follow Him, but our willingness. Paul knew the same thing about the Philippians. He was about to address their willingness in a most profound way. So, first, he affirmed their spiritual status and ability, and then he wrote verse 2.

Unity: The Central Characteristic of Christians (Phil. 2:2)

Then make my joy complete: be unified. This would have been the simple way to say what Paul wanted to say, but it would also have been far less emotional, less dramatic, and less effective. Paul said, **Make my joy complete by being like-minded, having the same love, being one is spirit and purpose** (v. 2). Paul knew that the answer to the Philippians' struggles was unity.

Unity is a recurring theme in Paul's writings. He seemed to consider unity the central characteristic of Christians. Disunity, or division, is from the Enemy. Christians who are estranged from one another are also estranged from Christ and vice versa. Paul warned the Philippians not to succumb to division. He described a unity of the deepest degree—the same unity for which Jesus prayed in John 17:22–23.

Humility: The Sign of Unity (Phil. 2:3–4)

In these verses, Paul hinted that the level of humility in the Philippian church would tell them the level of unity. If we succeed in unity, the result will be humility. However, if we lack unity, all that is left is selfishness. This truth is fully exposed in troubled times. During trials, it is tempting to look out only for our own interests. However, if we are unified as a body, we can sacrifice willingly for one another. If our church is merely a group of individuals who happen to be in the same place on Sunday mornings, then we have no church and trouble will divide us. Even success may divide us, for each individual will be tempted to look for personal glory and advantage during prosperous times.

Usually people think of humility as an individual act, and while it is, it is interesting to see that Paul related our ability to be humble with our willingness to be unified. That means we want our identity to be defined by the group, not by our individual character. As Christians, we should realize that the individual cannot be complete in isolation. Where we find unity is where we will find true humility. This can be a barrier to church growth. Visitors can tell the difference between genuine and false unity, genuine and false humility. Churches that want to reach out must be unified within.

Be Like Christ (Phil. 2:5-11)

Many scholars believe verses 6–11 are part of an early Christian hymn that was familiar to the Philippians. Here, Paul used it to illustrate his point that Christians, especially during times of trial, should be like Christ. It is not enough to simply say, "Be like Christ." It is necessary to explain what that means. Most of the time when this passage is preached, the focus is on Jesus and His relationship to God and humankind. While that is the content of the hymn, we must remember that Paul was using that content in the context of encouraging the Philippians so they can persevere in their trouble—if they become like Christ. Paul seemed to have structured the first four verses of this chapter (unity, humility, and self-sacrifice) to parallel the themes of verses 6–8.

WORDS FROM WESLEY

Philippians 2:5

He to whom this character belongs, and he alone, is a Christian. To him the one, eternal, omnipresent, all-perfect Spirit, is the "Alpha and Omega, the first and the last"; not his Creator only, but his Sustainer, his Preserver, his Governor; yea, his Father, his Saviour, Sanctifier, and Comforter. This God is his God, and his All, in time and in eternity. . . .

Let all therefore that desire to please God condescend to be taught of God, and take care to walk in that path which God himself hath appointed. . . . And see that you begin where God himself begins: "Thou shalt have no other gods before me." Is not this the first, our Lord himself being the Judge, as well as the great, commandment? First, therefore, see that ye love God; next, your neighbour—every child of man. From this fountain let every temper, every affection, every passion flow. So shall that "mind be in you which was also in Christ Jesus." Let all your thoughts, words, and actions spring from this! So shall you "inherit the kingdom prepared for you from the beginning of the world." (WJW, vol. 7, 272–273)

The hymn begins with the assertion that Jesus is in essential unity with God. For those who say the Bible never speaks directly of the Trinity, this verse seems to assume its existence. Jesus (the Son) and God (the Father) are presented as distinct persons, yet eternally unified. Though Jesus was divine (unified with God), He **did not consider** His **equality** (distinct person) **with God** (v. 6) as though it were something He should hold on to at any cost. The hymn wants us to understand that the entire work of Jesus is based on His foundational unity with the Father. So our work as Christians must be based on our unity with one another. Too many times Christians seem only concerned with their relationship with God and neglect their relationships with other Christians, or rationalize ill feelings they have for other Christians, as if the two relationships were separate. Unless we are unified, we are impotent in the power of the Spirit.

WORDS FROM WESLEY

Philippians 2:6

Who being in the essential *form*, the incommunicable nature of God from eternity (as He was afterward in the form of man, real God, as real man), *counted it no act of robbery* (that is the precise meaning of the words), no invasion of another's prerogative, but His own strict and unquestionable right, *to be equal with God*. The word here translated *equal*, occurs in the adjective form, five or six times in the New Testament: Matthew 20:12; Luke 6:34; John 5:18; Acts 11:17; Revelation 21:16. In all which places it expresses not a bare resemblance, but a real and proper equality. It here implies both the fullness and the supreme height of the godhead; to which are opposed, *he emptied*, and He *humbled himself*. (ENNT)

Jesus' divine unity was of such a nature that He could be utterly self-sacrificial. Most of the time when we think of the sacrifice of Christ, we think of the cross. This hymn asks us to think more broadly. The incarnation itself was an extreme act of self-sacrifice. Jesus **made himself nothing, taking the very nature of a servant, being made in human likeness** (v. 7). It is very important for Paul's argument that Jesus is the one taking the action here. Notice that God did not make Jesus do anything. Jesus voluntarily made himself nothing. In the ancient world, servants were considered property, not people. They had no rights, no expectations of life, liberty, or the pursuit of anything. The hymn equates humanity with slavery because everyone dies and so death is master over all. Just as the servant has no choice but to obey the master, every human being has no choice but to die. Jesus, however, had a choice and He chose death—but why?

Remember, the Philippians were in distress and Paul was holding up this hymn as a pattern for dealing with trouble. Jesus chose death in response to trouble, but not His own trouble, our trouble. Jesus knew we were enslaved to sin and death and could not free ourselves. He knew the only path to freedom must be made and marked by Him. He chose to die to give us a chance to live—but how?

Righteousness can never be defeated, because righteousness is always obedient to God. If Jesus chose death, God would reward that choice with life. Self-sacrifice is the ultimate expression of faith. Think of Abraham taking Isaac up to Mount Moriah. Abraham knew God would provide the sacrifice. Somehow, some way, Abraham knew if he gave himself up to death, which is what the giving of Isaac represented, God would give him life. Jesus, being in very nature God, knew full well that any sacrifice He made to death would be followed by the power of the resurrection. That is why He told the Jews if they destroyed the temple (His body), He would build it again in three days.

WORDS FROM WESLEY

Philippians 2:8

And being found in fashion as a man—A common man, without any peculiar excellence or comeliness, *he humbled himself*—To a still greater depth, *becoming obedient*—To God, though equal with Him, *even unto death*—The greatest instance both of humiliation and obedience, *yea, the death of the cross*—Inflicted on few but servants or slaves. (ENNT)

Not only did God grant life in the resurrection, but also victory. **Therefore God exalted him to the highest place and gave him the name that is above every name, that at the name of Jesus every knee should bow** (vv. 9–10). The message to the Philippians was that their suffering was righteous suffering; therefore if they were unified, humble, and self-sacrificial, God would give them victory, not simply earthly victory but heavenly and eternal victory, a victory that triumphs over death itself. If we approach life as Jesus did, then we will receive life as Jesus did.

WORDS FROM WESLEY

Philippians 2:10

That every knee—That divine honour might be paid in every possible manner by every creature, *might bow*—Either with love or trembling, *of those in heaven, earth, under the earth*—That is, through the whole universe. (ENNT)

In other writings, Paul referred to the Christian life as the resurrected life. He meant to say that the Christian will experience victory over sin in this life. A life without victory would be a resuscitated life, not a resurrected life. A resuscitated life is still dominated by death and will eventually be taken. A resurrected life is a life lived in unity with Christ, in fellowship with the Spirit, and in unity with fellow Christians.

It is never more important to live the resurrected life than in times of trouble. This is when our testimony becomes clear to everyone, believers and nonbelievers alike. In times of trouble, let us remember Paul's message to the Philippians in these eleven verses. Let us focus on our faith and not on ourselves. May we unify our hearts and minds. May we humble and sacrifice ourselves, exercising our faith that God is the giver of life and that once He gives life, nothing, "neither death nor life, neither angels nor demons, neither the present nor the future, nor any powers, neither height nor depth, nor anything else in all creation, will be able to separate us from the love of God that is in Christ Jesus our Lord" (Rom. 8:38–39). May we be like Christ.

DISCUSSION

It is not uncommon for talented people to boast, so we may wonder if humility is a lost or devalued virtue. Reflect on how to determine whether humility is a strength or weakness.

1. Who did Paul cite as the supreme example of humility?

2. How do you distinguish false humility (which is actually pride) from true humility?

3. What do you think the response or reaction would be at your place of employment to a Christian who followed in Jesus' steps?

4. If someone advised you to look in a mirror every morning and say, "I love you," how would you respond?

5. Can a humble person ever be too big for a small ministry? Explain your answer.

6. When Jesus came to earth, He assumed the role of a servant, but did He cease to be God? Defend your answer.

7. How will you demonstrate an attitude of selfless service on behalf of a fellow Christian this week?

8. How might a Christian with a humble attitude diffuse a potential explosive situation at church?

PRAYER

Father God, You who gave our Lord the name "Jesus" and exalted Him, teach us that humility begins with obedience.

8

KEEP ON GROWING

Philippians 2:12–30

Our relationship with God and other believers must be nurtured.

When you were a kid in school, what did you and your classmates do when the teacher left the room for several minutes? Did you keep on working or goof off? What should believers do, knowing Jesus is physically absent but will return someday? Should we spend our days in idle conduct, or should we keep on growing spiritually?

This study focuses on the spiritual growth Paul encouraged in the lives of the Philippian believers. Although he was absent from them, he summoned them to maintain a strong missionary outreach and stand shoulder to shoulder with God's appointed leaders. As you work through this study, you will feel compelled to keep on keeping on.

COMMENTARY

This section picks up and continues Paul's thought from 1:27–28. It is helpful to read 2:12–30, especially 12–13, immediately after 1:27–28. The context of this thought is Paul's imprisonment, which was potentially psychologically devastating to the Philippians. Paul wanted to make sure the Philippians placed their trust in God and not in him. It is so easy for us to place our faith in another person, especially a person of high character and spirituality. This is always a mistake because then the circumstances of others can fundamentally affect our faith. In the case of the Philippians, Paul's imprisonment could give them a sense of spiritual failure and defeat. However, if they understand that it is God who works in them and not Paul, their faith can stand firm.

It is true that we can use others as role models. Paul even told the Philippians, "Whatever you have learned or received or heard from me, or seen in me—put it into practice. And the God of peace will be with you" (4:9). Our task is to keep two truths in force and in balance: (1) We need other Christians to live our Christian lives; (2) our total dependence must be on God alone. This is yet another paradox of Christianity, and it is the one Paul addressed in this section, which is a personal and passionate letter within the letter.

Obedience Is for God, Not People (Phil. 2:12–13)

If trouble comes upon us because we are being obedient to God, we may wonder why we should continue to be obedient. Paul was obedient to God, and the Philippians witnessed first-hand his beating and imprisonment. Now that Paul was in prison in Rome, his death seemed imminent. One of the best ways to encourage someone is to point out past successes. Paul reminded the Philippians of their habit of obedience whether he was present or absent. The Philippians were not like the Corinthians, who could not maintain obedience when Paul was away. The Corinthians obeyed Paul, but never grew in their faith. The Philippians obeyed God through Paul and grew in their spirituality.

WORDS FROM WESLEY

Philippians 2:12

But what are the steps which the Scriptures direct us to take, in the working out of our own salvation? . . . Carefully avoid every evil word and work; yea, abstain from all appearance of evil. And "learn to do well": Be zealous of good works, of works of piety, as well as works of mercy; family prayer, and crying to God in secret. Fast in secret, and "your Father which seeth in secret, He will reward you openly." "Search the Scriptures": Hear them in public, read them in private, and meditate therein. At every opportunity, be a partaker of the Lord's Supper. "Do this in remembrance" of Him; and He will meet you at His own table. Let your conversation be with the children of God; and see that it "be in grace, seasoned with salt." As ye have time, do good unto all men; to their souls and to their bodies. And herein "be ye steadfast, unmovable, always abounding in the work of the Lord." It then only remains, that ye deny yourselves and take up your cross daily. Deny yourselves every pleasure which does not prepare you for taking pleasure in God, and willingly embrace every means of drawing near to God, though it be a cross, though it be grievous to flesh and blood. (WJW, vol. 6, 510–511)

Paul pointed the Philippians to their continued obedience, particularly in his absence, to show them that God is in control. God is the one working in them to produce such consistent obedience. He will continue to work in them if they remain focused on the central issue of their faith—their salvation. By urging the Philippians to **continue** working out their **salvation with fear and trembling** (v. 12), Paul was communicating at least two concepts: death is not the end, and they are not dead. In other words, Paul subtly acknowledged the reality of their fear that he might be killed, but he reminded them that salvation is salvation from death; it is hope of eternal life. He also gently reminded them that even if he died, God still had work for them to do. Christianity will not end with the death of Paul. The gospel goes beyond any one person or group of people. Out task is not to predict the future, but to live in the present by the power of the Spirit, continuing to work out the implications of our own salvation amid any circumstance. Our dependence must be on God.

WORDS FROM WESLEY
Philippians 2:13

If God worketh in you, then work out your own salvation. The original word, rendered *work out*, implies the doing a thing thoroughly. *Your own*; for you yourselves must do this, or it will be left undone for ever. Your *own salvation*: Salvation begins with what is usually termed (and very properly) *preventing grace*; including the first wish to please God, the first dawn of light concerning His will, and the first slight transient conviction of having sinned against Him. . . . Salvation is carried on by *convincing grace*, usually in Scripture termed *repentance*; which brings a larger measure of self-knowledge, and a farther deliverance from the heart of stone. Afterwards we experience the proper Christian salvation; whereby, "through grace," we "are saved by faith"; consisting of those two grand branches, justification and sanctification. By justification we are saved from the guilt of sin, and restored to the favour of God; by sanctification we are saved from the power and root of sin, and restored to the image of God. All experience, as well as Scripture, show this salvation to be both instantaneous and gradual. It begins the moment we are justified, in the holy, humble, gentle, patient love of God and man. It gradually increases from that moment, . . . till, in another instant, the heart is cleansed from all sin, and filled with pure love to God and man. But even that love increases more and more, till we "grow up in all things into Him that is our Head"; till we attain "the measure of the stature of the fullness of Christ." (WJW, vol. 6, 509)

Rejoice in the Faith That Produces Eternal Holiness (Phil. 2:14–18)

In these verses, Paul continued to acknowledge the reality of his possible execution. He did not degrade the Philippians for their fear, nor did he rebuke them for anticipating their mourning. He did, however, redirect their thoughts. He began by summarizing his teaching to the Philippians in a few short lines: **Do everything without complaining or arguing, so that you may become blameless and pure, children of God without fault in a crooked and depraved generation, in which you shine like stars in the universe as you hold out the word of life** (vv. 14–16).

This amazing summation is not only meant to recall Paul's entire teaching and ministry to their minds, but also to remind them of their own successful ministry so far and the heights to which God has called them. Paul had been instrumental in their spiritual lives. If it were not for Paul, the Philippians would not have been reached when they were, and some of the believers may not have ever converted. However, Paul wanted the Philippians to realize exactly what the gospel had done in them. They were shining stars in a dark world. They did hold out the Word of Life to save people who were dying. These things were to continue, as they have, even if Paul was executed. If these activities were to cease, then Paul would have labored in vain. As it is, Paul had every reason to boast in his faith and in the Philippians. Their faith was living proof of his own faith. True faith produces faith in others because true faith is communicated through the faithful by the power of the Spirit.

Paul's ultimate goal in his ministry was to communicate his faith in a way that created an avenue for the work of the Spirit. Whatever happened to him, **even if** he was **poured out like a drink offering** (v. 17), the continuance of the faith was his victory. A drink offering was significant in a desert region with little means of transporting and holding water. A drink offering poured out on the sand represented a life totally sacrificed to God. As the sand quickly soaked in the water, the drink offering also signified the brevity and fragility of human life. How quickly we pass and how quickly we may be forgotten, but our life of faith affects the eternity of generations to come.

WORDS FROM WESLEY

Philippians 2:17

Yea, and if I be offered, literally, *if I be poured out upon the sacrifice of your faith*—The *Philippians*, as the other converted heathens, were a sacrifice to God through St. Paul's ministry (Rom. 15:16). And as in sacrificing, wine was poured at the foot of the altar, so he was willing that his blood should be poured out. The expression well agrees with that kind of martyrdom, by which he was afterward offered up to God. (ENNT)

Paul said even if he died and was forgotten tomorrow, he rejoiced to know that his life rested in the faith of his dear Philippian friends. He looked at his prison cell and his possible execution as evidence that his faith in Christ through his suffering would encourage the Philippian Christians to look to God in their times of trouble. For this, Paul rejoiced. He rejoiced to know that God could use even his death to promote life, that nothing can stop the force of his faith from preaching the gospel. It will continue through the Philippians. For this, he encouraged the Philippians to rejoice with him. If his race was almost over, this meant he was nearly home. It meant he had been faithful and would receive the reward of the faithful. In heaven, that reward is eternal life. On earth, his reward was the continuing faith of the Philippians.

We can learn a lot about how we should live our lives from these verses. It is not important that we leave a legacy of money or success or invention or even curing disease. The important legacy is the legacy of faith. We should live so that even though we are forgotten, those who follow us will have the Word of Life branded on their hearts and will pass it on. Even this we do not for ourselves, but for the glory of God.

Passing the Spiritual Torch (Phil. 2:19-30)

These twelve verses best illustrate how Paul balanced the need for other Christians with the total dependence on God. He knew that all of his encouragement to the Philippians could not replace personal contact. The gospel message is inherently communal. You cannot truly give the message without giving yourself. Paul knew this as well as anyone. He also knew he could not go personally, so he would **send Timothy** (v. 19), his son in the faith.

Sending Timothy had several implications. First, Paul was showing the Philippians how much he wanted to go to them. In the ancient world, sending your son had the cultural impact of going yourself. It was an acceptable way to be in two places at once. It signified that the business you had there was as important as the business you were conducting where you were. We see this in the language Paul used to described Timothy as one with **genuine interest** in the **welfare** (v. 20) of the Philippians. Therefore, Paul had no need to write that he was **confident in the Lord** (v. 24) that he himself would **come** to them **soon**, except that Paul once again went beyond cultural expectations to embrace the fullness of what it meant to be human. As we minister to others, especially to other believers, we must make it a point to go beyond expectations. Our goal is to show the immeasurable worth of people, both to us and to God.

Second, sending Timothy was at least symbolic (if not literal) of Paul giving up his life for the Philippians. Ancient prisons were not equipped to care for prisoners. People on the outside had to provide food, water, clothing, medicine, and anything else the prisoner needed. Timothy would have been Paul's lifeline. There were probably others who would care for Paul, but none would be as diligent **as a son with his father** (v. 22). By sending Timothy, Paul was telling the Philippians that he would gladly give his life for them. He said he would send Timothy as soon as he saw how things went with him, not to delay sending Timothy, but that Timothy might be able to answer the questions Paul knew the Philippians would ask: "Is he going to trial? Will he be released? What are the exact charges?"

Perhaps it would be better to translate verse 25 as, "Also I think it is necessary." In addition to sending Timothy, Paul was sending back Epaphroditus, who came from Philippi with a letter from the Philippians and for the express purpose of caring for Paul. Paul was holding nothing back in his commitment to the Philippians. His total dependence was on God, so he could willingly sacrifice everything for his fellow believers. He needed them, but he also gave himself up for them.

Epaphroditus' illness would have been disappointing to the Philippians who sent him to take care of Paul. Paul sent him back to show the goodness and mercy of God. When Epaphroditus returned, Paul would have less anxiety because the Philippians would receive comfort. The lesson here is that when we share our blessings with others, we reduce our own anxiety by reducing the general anxiety of people who live in a fallen world.

Paul knew well the value of others and the sovereignty of God. For him, the two were indivisible. May God grant us the same faith.

DISCUSSION

Relationships can be thorny and jagged at times, but they can also be smooth and beautiful. The difference usually depends on what we bring to a relationship.

1. Why is it so important for church members to be friendly to one another? Why is it important for them to be friendly to the lost?

2. The Lord is the best friend anyone can have. How have you been cultivating your friendship with the Lord recently?

3. Do you need to spend more time with the Lord? How will you make or protect the time you spend with the Lord?

4. How is working out salvation vastly different from working for salvation?

5. Why should working out one's salvation make a Christian fear and tremble?

6. Paul mentored Timothy. As a result, Timothy had become an effective minister of the gospel. Think of a fellow believer you might disciple. How will you disciple that person?

7. What qualities in Timothy's life do you wish to emulate?

8. What qualities in Epaphroditus's life do you wish to emulate?

9. In what ways are you serving others as a brother or sister? A coworker? A fellow soldier? If you believe you fall short in these areas, how will you begin today to be a more faithful brother or sister, coworker, and soldier?

10. How might you motivate fellow church members to honor the pastor for his or her ministry on your behalf? What form of honor might you suggest?

PRAYER

Dear Lord, never let us settle into a spiritual rut. Rather, spur us on to good works that will allow Your holiness to shine through our lives in this dark world.

9

REACHING FOR THE GOAL

Philippians 3:1—4:4

Nothing is more important than pursuing life's ultimate goal.

A wise person observed that past experiences should be guideposts, not hitching posts. Christians should not live in the past. The Christian race is a marathon, and considerable distance still lies ahead before we cross the finish line. As the apostle Paul ran the Christian race, he refused to rest on his laurels. Like a dedicated runner, he stretched every muscle and pushed his body to the limit to cross the finish line and receive "the prize for which God has called me heavenward in Christ Jesus" (Phil. 3:14).

This study will motivate you to follow Paul's example. It will help you to value the prize Paul identified, and it will cheer you on as you reach for the goal.

COMMENTARY

In Philippians 3, Paul digressed abruptly from his subject matter in chapters 1 and 2. In the first two chapters, we see how Paul loved and appreciated these dear Christians and wanted Christ's best for them. But Paul knew how easily they could be led astray if they weren't careful. So now, as he contemplated sending Timothy to them, he realized warnings were in order.

Warning against Legalism (Phil. 3:1-9)

Paul was probably referring to the Judaizers, a group of Jewish Christians who perverted the gospel by advocating the necessity of circumcision and adherence to other Old Testament rituals for salvation, when he spoke of those **dogs** and those **men who do evil** in verse 2. In a play on words, Paul called these men **mutilators of the flesh** (*katatome*, to cut down or off) because of their insistence on circumcision (*peritome*, literally "to cut around"). Paul explained, **it is we who are the circumcision** (v. 3). The physical sign of circumcision was merely an outward sign of the inward work God had done in the hearts of His people. Paul further explained that being a "Jew" was not really about the physical rite of circumcision at all; his readers were the true circumcision, the true people of God, the true Israel, because of the circumcision of their hearts. The true Jews are **we who worship by the Spirit of God** as opposed to by human laws and **who glory in Christ Jesus** (v. 3).

WORDS FROM WESLEY

Philippians 3:4

For we can hardly conceive any who was more highly favoured with all the gifts both of nature and education. Besides his natural abilities, probably not inferior to those of any person then upon the earth, he had all the benefits of learning, studying at the University of Tarsus, afterwards brought up at the feet of Gamaliel, a person of the greatest account, both for knowledge and integrity, that was then in the whole Jewish nation. And he had all the possible advantages of religious education, being a Pharisee, the son of a Pharisee, trained up in the very straitest sect or profession, distinguished from all others by a more eminent strictness. And herein he had "profited above many" others, "who were his equals" in years, "being more abundantly zealous" of whatever he thought would please God, and "as touching the righteousness of the law, blameless." But it could not be, that he should hereby attain this simplicity and godly sincerity. It was all but lost labour; in a deep, piercing sense of which he was at length constrained to cry out, "The things which were gain to me, those I counted loss for Christ: Yea, doubtless, and I count all things but loss, for the excellency of the knowledge of Christ Jesus my Lord" (Phil. 3:7, 8). (WJW, vol. 5, 140)

The problem with legalism—demanding obedience to a list of laws to ensure salvation—is that it amounts to placing our **confidence in the flesh** (v. 3), in our own works. Paul adopted the argument of the Judaizers to show that he, of all people, had **reasons for such confidence** (v. 4). He was **circumcised on the eighth day** (v. 5), an indication of the higher status of a born Jew; he was **of the people of Israel**, meaning he was a native of Palestine. He was **of the tribe of Benjamin**, a true Jew. In fact, he was a **Hebrew of Hebrews** (v. 5); Hebrew was his native tongue and he was born of Hebrew parents. But these reasons for confidence were outside Paul's control. They were his heritage. Paul did choose to become **a Pharisee**, a meticulous keeper of God's law. He summed up his works in verse 6: **as for zeal, persecuting the church; as for legalistic righteousness, faultless.** You simply couldn't be a better "Jew" than Paul was.

WORDS FROM WESLEY

Philippians 3:12

Christian perfection, therefore, does not imply (as some men seem to have imagined) an exemption either from ignorance, or mistake, or infirmities, or temptations. Indeed, it is only another term for holiness. They are two names for the same thing. Thus, every one that is holy is, in the Scripture sense, perfect. Yet we may, Lastly, observe, that neither in this respect is there any absolute perfection on earth. There is no *perfection of degrees*, as it is termed; none which does not admit of a continual increase. So that how much soever any man has attained, or in how high a degree soever he is perfect, he hath still need to "grow in grace," and daily to advance in the knowledge and love of God his Saviour. (WJW, vol. 6, 5)

But none of those works of righteousness can save us. Paul said, **Whatever was to my profit I now consider loss for the sake of Christ** (v. 7). In fact, he considered **everything a loss** and **rubbish**

(v. 8; "food scraps" or "dung," either of which might have been enjoyed by **dogs**, v. 2) compared to knowing Christ. Paul was not saying the law was useless or rubbish, but putting one's trust in the law for righteousness was a poor substitute for embracing the Lord of righteousness. God provides a **righteousness that comes from God and is by faith** (v. 9).

Warning against Lawlessness (Phil. 3:18-19)

The Judaizers erred by overemphasizing the law to ensure salvation, but others took the opposite approach, focusing so much on "faith" that they actually embraced lawlessness. Paul appears to be addressing such people in 3:18–19. Their behavior drove Paul to **tears** as he watched them **live as enemies of the cross of Christ** (v. 18). To consciously and deliberately live a life of sin is to completely repudiate the cross of Christ. For those who do so, **their destiny is destruction**, and **their god is their stomach** (v. 19), meaning they are controlled by fleshly appetites. **Their glory is in their shame** (v. 19). They take pride in things of which they should be ashamed. Instead of having their minds on the things of God and His requirements, **their mind is on earthly things** (v. 19). Paul warned his readers that both those who put their confidence in their good works and those who have simply cast off restraint are missing the mark. Legalism and lawlessness, though opposites, both lead to the same end. God's people must be vigilant in not wavering to the left or to the right.

The Secret to Standing Firm (Phil. 3:10-17, 20-21; 4:1-4)

Interspersed throughout this chapter is Paul's secret to ensuring we are trusting only in Christ for our righteousness and living in a way that pleases Him.

Know Christ. Paul wanted **to know Christ and the power of his resurrection** (3:10). He wanted to have an intimate knowledge of Him in a personal relationship, not just an intellectual understanding. Coming to Christ means we have the power to overcome temptation and live a transcendent life, a life of commitment to know by experience **the fellowship of sharing in his sufferings** (v. 10). When we truly know Christ, we don't shrink from persecution. In fact, knowing Him means we *will* be hated and persecuted (Matt. 10:22–24). Paul had been told at the beginning of his ministry that suffering awaited him (Acts 9:16; see the fulfillment in 2 Cor. 11:24–27). And he counted it a privilege to be able to suffer for Christ. Paul's readers had also experienced such suffering.

Knowing Christ means we become **like him in his death** (Phil. 3:10). Paul certainly had in mind here dying to self and sin. Physical suffering has a way of teaching us what is important in life; it purifies and refines us, drawing our hearts toward Christ. Knowing Christ means experiencing His power in our lives to die to sin and selfishness.

Keep Your Eyes on the Goal. Paul concluded in verse 11: **and so, somehow, to attain to the resurrection from the dead.** Paul was not sure how he would attain to this resurrection, whether through his death or through the second coming of Christ. It little matters which. He confessed he had not **already obtained all this**; he had not **already been made perfect** (v. 12), but he was confident that it awaited him. He trusted in God's promises. He would **press on toward the goal to win the prize for which God has called** him **heavenward in Christ Jesus** (v. 14). The "prize" and **that for which Christ Jesus took hold of me** (v. 12) is certainly everlasting life in heaven. The Christian life is one of constant growth. We are always becoming more and more like Christ, but our knowledge of Him is never fully realized until we see Him face-to-face.

One thing I do, Paul said, **forgetting what is behind and straining toward what is ahead, I press on** (vv. 13–14), which implies work and great effort. Not that he had to work his way to heaven, but he had to struggle to stay the course. The imagery is that of a race in which the runner must be resolute and focused on the goal. A runner will never win the race if he or she is constantly looking backward. Paul made it his priority to forget what is behind. This is key to standing firm in our Christian faith. We need to let go of past failures and mistakes and not allow ourselves to be held captive by guilt or regrets. But we also must be willing to forget our past successes and accomplishments. The Christian faith must be lived in the present tense, with our eyes firmly fixed on what is to come.

WORDS FROM WESLEY

Philippians 3:14

Do you "walk by faith?" Observe the question. I do not ask, whether you curse, or swear, or profane the Sabbath, or live in any outward sin. I do not ask, whether you do good, more or less; or attend all the ordinances of God. But, suppose you are blameless in all these respects, I ask, in the name of God, by what standard do you judge of the value of things? By the visible or the invisible world? Bring the matter to an issue in a single instance. Which do you judge best—that your son should be a pious cobbler, or a profane lord? Which appears to you most eligible—that your daughter should be a child of God, and walk on foot, or a child of the Devil, and ride in a coach-and-six? When the question is concerning marrying your daughter, if you consider her body more than her soul, take knowledge of yourself: You are in the way to hell, and not to heaven; for you walk by sight, and not by faith. I do not ask, whether you live in any outward sin or neglect; but, do you *seek*, in the general tenor of your life, "the things that are above," or the things that are below? Do you "set your affection on things above," or on "things of the earth"? If on the latter, you are as surely in the way of destruction, as a thief or a common drunkard. My dear friends, let every man, every woman among you, deal honestly with yourselves. Ask your own heart, "What am I seeking day by day? What am I desiring? What am I pursuing? Earth or heaven? The things that are seen, or the things that are not seen?" What is your object. God or the world? As the Lord liveth, if the world is your object, still all your religion is vain. (WJW, vol. 7, 261–262)

In verses 20–21, Paul offered more incentive for keeping our eyes on the goal. He reminded us that **our citizenship is in heaven** (v. 20). Because we are aliens (strangers) in this world, our focus should always be on our heavenly home. Paul said, **we eagerly await a Savior from there** (v. 20) who **will transform our lowly bodies so that they will be like his glorious body** (v. 21). The hope of what is to come helps us to stand firm and to turn our gaze from the things of this world to the eternal.

WORDS FROM WESLEY

Philippians 3:21

Who will transform our vile body—Into the most perfect state, and the most beauteous form. It will then be purer than the unspotted firmament, brighter than the lustre of the stars: and which exceeds all parallel, which comprehends all perfection, *like unto his glorious body*—Like that wonderfully glorious body which He wears in His heavenly kingdom, and on His triumphant throne. (ENNT)

Live What You Already Know. Regarding Paul's comments so far, he said **all of us who are mature should take such a view of things** (v. 15). The mark of spiritual maturity is pressing on, not giving up when the going gets tough. It comes from keeping our eyes focused on the goal. Paul must have known there were some who disagreed with his conclusions, so he added, **if on some point you think differently, that too God will make clear to you** (v. 15). There is no more Paul could say to convince readers of the truth of his words. He trusted God to confirm it to their hearts.

We all have an obligation to **live up to what we have already attained** (v. 16). God's people should be obedient to what they understand. Paul's command, though, is not an excuse for living at a low level. What had the Philippians already attained? Salvation in Jesus Christ. They already had intimate knowledge of the

Savior and His righteousness and power. Living up to that was a high calling. We can't use lack of knowledge or understanding as an excuse; we know enough to live the kind of life God requires.

Follow the Example of Godly Christians. Paul entreated his readers to follow his example and to **take note of those who live according to the pattern we gave you** (v. 17). By following Paul's instructions in 3:7–16, young believers would be able to grow quickly to maturity, avoiding pitfalls along the way. They in turn would become models for others in their walk.

Therefore, said Paul, **that is how you should stand firm in the Lord** (4:1). Knowing Christ and seeking to become like Him, keeping our eyes on the goal, living what we know, and following the example of godly Christians is the secret for standing firm in Christ. With 4:1, we come to the end of Paul's "digression," but verses 2–3 show us a practical application of what Paul just taught. He made a plea to two women, **Euodia and ... Syntyche to agree with each other in the Lord** (v. 2). Paul requested help in this matter from a **loyal yokefellow** (v. 3). He urged this man to **help these women**. They had **contended at** Paul's **side in the cause of the gospel** (v. 3). They had done so much and now were accomplishing so little because of their disagreement.

If we could just learn to keep our focus on the goal and the prize, if we could just occupy ourselves with knowing Christ and becoming like Him, we would probably get rid of 90 percent of the fussing among people. Don't get sidetracked, said Paul. We're in a race. We need to run it with perseverance, not allowing anything to distract us.

Paul ended as he began, with the command to **rejoice in the Lord** (4:4; 3:1). Sometimes our trials and struggles threaten to steal our joy. When we take our eyes off our circumstances, however, and focus on the Lord, we can do little else than rejoice. He saves us and He can keep us! Rejoice!

DISCUSSION

Life is slipping away with every tick of the clock, and therefore there is less time to fulfill life's goals. But what matters most is to have a worthy goal.

1. How did Paul's goals change when he became a Christian? How did yours?

2. Why do religious credentials fail to help a person gain acceptance with God?

3. How would you explain the way of salvation to a lost, self-righteous person?

4. Do you think complacency characterizes many Christians? If so, what do you think is an effective cure for complacency?

5. What lesser things threaten to take our eyes of the goal of holiness? What keeps you focused on the goal?

6. Paul urged the Philippians to take note of godly believers. Who has set a good example for you to follow? What commendable qualities do you see in that person or those persons?

7. On what common ground did Paul appeal for unity between Euodia and Syntyche?

8. How might you help to reconcile two feuding believers?

9. How can you rejoice in spite of the perilous times we live in?

PRAYER

We pray, O Lord, that we might be drawn to Your purpose and goal for us. Take away any motive or desire that would keep us from becoming who You would have us be.

10

THE BENEFITS OF THE CHRISTIAN WALK

Philippians 4:5–23

There is nothing better than life in Christ.

What's so great about being a Christian? How would you answer this question? After all, troubles strike Christians as well as non-Christians. When unemployment rises, Christians as well as non-Christians find themselves out of work. Accidents injure Christians as well as non-Christians. Cancer and other serious diseases afflict Christians as well as non-Christians. So what's the big deal about being a Christian?

This study will help you answer these tough questions. As you study Philippians 4:5–23, you will discover and cherish the reality that God's peace is as near as a whispered prayer, His strength is available in every circumstance, and His promise to meet our every need is fully reliable. These benefits are priceless!

COMMENTARY

In the preceding verses, Paul gave his readers the sad word that people around them will not always act with ideal manners (3:18–19; 4:2; see also 1:28–29). When others let Christians down, how should we respond? We face at least two options. First, we could let self-consumed, quarrelsome people (3:19; 4:2) pull the church down to their level. The better choice is to respond with grace through Christ Jesus.

Paul's Suggestion: Be Proactive, Not Reactive (Phil. 4:5–9)

The last study finished describing the first of several ironic weapons: joy (4:4). In that same positive tone, Paul continued. **Let your gentleness be evident to all** (v. 5). How can joy and gentleness serve as weapons? When enemies realize they may be able to control people's possessions or even their bodies but cannot conquer their spirits, those enemies feel defeated. And Christians who find strength in the joy of the Lord, living like Jesus even amid disaster, cannot help but feel God has given victory.

How can Christians maintain a positive attitude amid discouraging circumstances? By remembering that **the Lord is near** (v. 5). This short sentence can speak two meanings. We can choose between them or firmly grasp both. Perhaps Paul pointed to Jesus' imminent return (1:6). Whatever God's people face, it will pass. God has won; there is no doubt. But also, God is present even now (4:9)—to hear His people pray and give them His peace. Those themes dominate verse 6: **Do not be anxious about anything, but in everything, by prayer and petition, with thanksgiving, present your requests to God.**

With these words, was Paul offering some sappy "paste a smile on your face and ignore life's problems" solution? No. Paul felt appropriate concern for hurting brothers and sisters (1:23–24; compare 2 Cor. 11:28). Later, Paul would affirm the Philippian church for its concern over his well-being (Phil. 4:10), and he would express his hope for their receiving what they needed (v. 19). At the same time, when Paul felt situations (his own or others' whom he loved) were outside his control, he could always find rest in the fact that the sovereign God had not gone off duty. Paul invited his readers to follow his own example in taking **requests to God** (v. 6). Would God always do what His servants wanted? No, Paul could not offer that false ideal. God's people remained His servants. He remained their Lord.

But they could always trust Him to do what is best. On that basis, every prayer could include **thanksgiving**.

God's **peace** will **guard** the **hearts and . . . minds** of His children (v. 7). As Paul wrote, he was a prisoner in Rome. Picture him chained to a Roman soldier. Paul was continually under guard to prevent his escape. In a similar way, God's peace guarded the Philippians, not to inhibit but to guarantee their freedom. Nothing or no one could approach them without God's consent. With God, kind of like a big brother around to protect, they could feel secure—living with a joyful, gentle, grateful spirit.

WORDS FROM WESLEY
Philippians 4:7

Another fruit of this living faith is peace. For, "being justified by faith," having all our sins blotted out, "we have peace with God, through our Lord Jesus Christ" (Rom. 5:1). This indeed our Lord himself, the night before His death, solemnly bequeathed to all His followers: "Peace," saith He, "I leave with you" (you who "believe in God," and "believe also in me"); "my peace I give unto you": "Not as the world giveth, give I unto you. Let not your heart be troubled, neither let it be afraid" (John 14:27). And again, "These things have I spoken unto you, that in me ye might have peace" (John 16:33). This is that "peace of God which passeth all understanding," that serenity of soul which it hath not entered into the heart of a natural man to conceive, and which it is not possible for even the spiritual man to utter. And it is a peace which all the powers of earth and hell are unable to take from him. Waves and storms beat upon it, but they shake it not; for it is founded upon a rock. (WJW, vol. 5, 216)

So on what should the Philippians (and we today) focus attention? The problems of the world? Christians can never ignore those in need. Instead, we live to serve them. At the same time, we concentrate primarily not on the hell from which we rescue others, but the heaven to which we invite them. **Finally, brothers,**

whatever is true, whatever is noble, whatever is right, whatever is pure, whatever is lovely, whatever is admirable—if anything is excellent or praiseworthy—think about such things (v. 8). This verse ends with its central command: **think**. With this word, Paul did not invite his readers merely to gather weekly to regain appropriate perspective. He wished their minds to be dominated by their memory of who God is, and who they were—in God.

WORDS FROM WESLEY

Philippians 4:8

I am persuaded they [three volumes of poems Wesley had dedicated to the Countess of Huntingdon] will not be unacceptable to you, were it only on this account—that many of them describe what a person of quality ought, and what I trust you desire, to be.

My heart's desire and prayer to God for you is, that you may never rest short of this: That "whatsoever things are true, whatsoever things are venerable, whatsoever things are just, whatsoever things are pure, whatsoever things are lovely, whatsoever things are honourable; if there be any virtue, if there be any praise, you may think on these things: And my God shall supply all your need, according to his riches in glory by Christ Jesus." (WJW, vol. 14, 331)

How did Paul conclude this paragraph? With a typical bit of emphasis. "Don't ignore this set of instructions; instead **put it into practice**" (v. 9). "Do what I say"—that's easy. But the apostle also stepped further onto a limb: "Do what I do." Let's assume that Lydia and others of Paul's first Philippian converts (Acts 16:14–15, 34, 40) still gathered with this church. Even if they had moved on, they had certainly shared their memories of Paul's first missionary visit to their city. The account of those early days and particularly one fateful night would have passed into the lore of that congregation.

After arrest in Philippi, Paul and Silas had been badly beaten for their faith, and then ruthlessly thrown into a dungeon. How did they respond? They offered their requests to God, doing so with songs of praise. In their cell, the two did not know what would happen next. But they lived for God even there. When an earthquake came, Paul recognized its source. Knowing God was near, Paul calmly maintained decorum in the prison; none of the prisoners rioted or even escaped. When the jailer pled for mercy, the two Christian prisoners gently offered him God's grace. The story of Paul's courage and witness is still told (Acts 16:22–34). On that basis, Paul could then reassure the Philippians: "If you stay as close to God as I have, then you will sense His presence. **The God of peace will be with you**" (Phil. 4:9).

Paul's Affirmation: You Have Shared Generously (Phil. 4:10-13)

Early in this new paragraph, Paul portrayed his own contentment in any type of circumstances (4:11–12). But once again, Paul had not moved into some stoical indifference. Like any human being, he preferred a pleasant state of affairs over pain. So, with true sincerity, he rejoiced in the Philippians' renewed **concern** for his comfort (v. 10). Through Epaphroditus, the Philippian church had sent him gifts (4:18; see also 2:25). In addition, the companionship of Epaphroditus had itself been a gift to Paul the prisoner (2:30).

At this point, Paul noted the Philippian church's previous lack of material support for Paul. He did this not to criticize them but to excuse them. At least during its earliest days, the Philippian church had sent Paul support—when he was in the neighboring city of Thessalonica (4:16). A bit later, some church(es) in Macedonia, perhaps the one in Philippi, had sent support to Paul in Corinth (2 Cor. 11:9). Why did the church not send support more regularly? Despite the fact that the Romans had developed an efficient postal system, letters still took weeks or months to be delivered. By the time letters from Paul could reach friends to let them know his current site of ministry, he likely had moved on. Also, sending a gift involved much more than popping a check in the mail. A messenger had to carry a potentially heavy load of coins from location to location. Even the travel of such a messenger was no simple matter. In this particular case, Epaphroditus, while traveling, fell ill and nearly died (2:26–27). Paul did not take for granted all the sacrifices involved in this gift. He expressed his gratitude for such generosity.

In case the Philippians somehow misread his motivation, thinking he was criticizing them for not giving sooner, Paul offered two verses of reassuring testimony. First, **I have learned to be content whatever the circumstances**, when **in need** or in **plenty** (4:11–12). Here Paul alluded to a characteristic treasured by many of his non-Christian contemporaries. Paul recognized that his sufficiency came not from himself, but from Jesus: **I can do everything** (in this context being content in all circumstances, only) **through him who gives me strength** (v. 13).

WORDS FROM WESLEY

Philippians 4:11

I have learned—From God. He only can teach this, *in every thing therewith to be content*—Joyfully and thankfully patient. Nothing less is Christian content. We may observe a beautiful gradation in the expressions: I have learned; I know; I am instructed; I can. (ENNT)

Paul's Proclamation: God Will Meet Your Needs (Phil. 4:14–20)

This next paragraph sounds quite like any number of thank-you notes—at least until 4:19, where Paul spoke extraordinary words. There he gave the Philippians more than thanks for their gift. He promised an even better gift in return: God's supply of their every need. Note how he built up to this climactic moment.

Paul moved toward 4:19's great promise by offering some implied conditions for this oft-quoted promise. No, Paul did not directly offer conditions, saying something like, "*If* you are generous, God will meet all your needs." That would sound like a guilt-inducing moralism. Instead, before giving the promise Paul highlighted the uniqueness of his relationship with this individual congregation.

Of course, Paul lovingly cared for each church he founded. Even so, he received a variety of responses. On one extreme, we have the Corinthian church, which, at times, undermined Paul's ministry. Many churches neither opposed nor did much to support Paul. But then there's the church at Philippi. Paul highlighted the special place these people had in his heart (1:7–8; 4:1). And the strength of this relationship was mutual. Several times in this letter's first chapter, Paul alluded to this group as his "partner," noting how its members freely shared his life and circumstances (see 1:5, 7, 30).

WORDS FROM WESLEY
Philippians 4:13

I can do all things—Even fulfill all the will of God. (ENNT)

And of course in this paragraph, Paul noted that the Philippians, unlike all other churches (4:15), **sent** Paul **aid again and again when** he **was in need** (v. 16). This particular letter thanked the Philippians for the latest installment in their ongoing gift, one sent with **Epaphroditus** (v. 18). Paul certainly rejoiced in what he received, but to an even greater degree, he celebrated the love and spiritual depth of the Philippian church. He compared the gift with **a fragrant offering, an acceptable sacrifice,**

pleasing to God (v. 18). Paul's picture involves an offering of sweet-smelling incense to God (see Ex. 30:1). In effect, the apostle pointed out that, although the Philippians had sent money to him in Rome, they had in reality given their gift to God (compare Matt. 25:40).

Paul wanted to respond in kind. He could not send material gifts, but he could write a letter, offering in return all he and his God could give: **My God will meet all your needs according to his glorious riches in Christ Jesus** (Phil. 4:19). Can all Christians easily claim this verse, or does its promise imply conditions? God is by no means stingy, but this promise may belong especially to those Christians who throw themselves on God, who hold back none of their possessions from His use.

As he considered God's generosity to and through His people, Paul could not hold back from giving praise: **To our God and Father be glory for ever and ever. Amen** (v. 20).

Paul's Farewell: Greetings and Grace (Phil. 4:21–23)

The letter closes with warm greetings all the way around. Paul sent his own best wishes, as well those from other Christians around him. He closed his letter with "greetings" from Jesus Christ himself, who continually offers His grace to all His people.

DISCUSSION

Does it really pay to serve Jesus? More than one Christian has asked this question when troubles engulfed him or her.

1. Paul declared the Lord is near. Why do you agree or disagree that He is near even when you do not feel His presence?

2. Is God interested in all our concerns? Is any "problem" too small to present to Him in prayer? Why or why not?

3. How might it help you pray more effectively if you thanked God for past evidences of His care?

4. How do you know from personal experience that God's peace transcends all understanding?

5. Why do you agree or disagree that what we program into our minds influences how we live? Is it right to think evil thoughts if we do not put them into action? Why or why not?

6. Is prosperity a sign of spirituality? Why or why not?

7. How is it possible to be content when money is tight?

8. The Philippians gave consistently and sacrificially to support their missionary Paul. Why do you agree or disagree that tithing may represent sacrificial giving?

9. Why do you agree or disagree that God has promised to meet our needs but not our wants?

10. How might you encourage a fellow believer who has recently lost his or her job?

PRAYER

Lord, You give us strength to do everything. Show us what You want us to do, and help us to do it.

11

THE SUPREMACY OF CHRIST

Colossians 1:15–20, 27

Christ is supreme over all and sufficient for all.

Jesus asked His disciples who people said He was. They reported that some said He was John the Baptist; some said He was Elijah; and others said He was Jeremiah or one of the prophets. And then Jesus asked who the disciples believed He was. Without hesitation, Peter pronounced, "You are the Christ, the Son of the living God" (Matt. 16:16). He spoke the truth with deep conviction, and Jesus commended him for doing so.

Our faith and lifestyle depend upon a correct understanding of who Jesus is. This study will present Jesus as Peter correctly viewed Him—the Son of the living God. Let us honor and worship Him for who He is.

COMMENTARY

The apostle Paul wrote this letter (Col. 1:1) to the "holy and faithful brothers in Christ at Colosse" (1:2). Paul had not met these Christians, but he had heard about them from Epaphras (1:4, 7–8). Epaphras was a native of Colosse, a leader in the church, and possibly its organizer (4:12–13). The church in Colosse was probably established during Paul's extended ministry in Ephesus (Acts 19:1–10).

This letter to the Colossians is one of the Prison Epistles, which means it was written while Paul was "in chains" (Col. 4:3). While it is obvious that this letter was written by Paul from a Roman prison, we don't know for certain which imprisonment it was (2 Cor. 11:23). It may be that Paul was in Rome waiting for his trial before Caesar (Acts 28:16–31).

The letters to the Ephesians, Philippians, and Colossians all contain passages that give sweeping descriptions of Jesus Christ. Along with John 1 and Hebrews 1–2, these passages tell us who Christ is in no uncertain terms. The supremacy of Christ over everything in heaven and on earth must have been a great encouragement to the imprisoned apostle.

This letter was written to answer some errors that had crept into the church. Epaphras apparently had gone to Paul for help in dealing with the false teachers who were misleading some of the Colossians. The errors at Colosse were a result of syncretism, combining ideas and practices from several religions to create a supposed better way to God. This "salad bar" approach to spirituality apparently led some to combine Greek philosophy, Jewish rituals, ancient cultic practices, and Christianity. The basic idea behind these errors was that God is inaccessible to humans. Layers of angels and lesser deities separate Him from us. These spiritual beings would assist humans in their search for God if the individuals knew and did the right things. These teachers believed Jesus was one of the spiritual beings who wanted to help us connect with God. However, they supposed He simply could not do it all by himself.

Paul pointed these straying Christians back to the true gospel. Colossians 1:15–20 may have been an early Christian hymn, and Paul used it to underscore Christ's incomparability in all things. Christ is over all creation (vv. 15–17). He holds first place in our redemption from sin and death (vv. 18–20). Paul also spotlights how God has reconciled "all things, whether things on earth or things in heaven, by making peace through [Christ's] blood, shed on the cross" (v. 20). This is the genuine, history-changing good news for which we all have been waiting.

He Is the Image of the Invisible God (Col. 1:15)

He is the visible manifestation of God. **Image** translates the Greek word from which we get the English word *icon*. An icon can be an emblem or sign. It can be a symbol of something or it can be an accurate representation of it. Paul used this word to say Jesus Christ makes **the invisible God** understandable and knowable to us. Since God is Spirit, He is **invisible** to our physical eyes, in that He is beyond our grasp and knowledge. However, God has bridged the chasm that separated us from Him in Christ, who **is the image of the invisible God** (v. 15).

We don't need some secret wisdom or angelic assistance to reach God. He came to us in Jesus Christ. When a person meets Christ, he or she has met God. Jesus Christ is all we need to know God.

WORDS FROM WESLEY

Colossians 1:15

Who is—By describing the glory of Christ and the pre-eminence over the highest angels, the apostle here lays a foundation for the reproof of all worshipers of angels: *the image of the invisible God*—Whom none can represent but His only begotten Son: in His divine nature, the invisible image, in His human, the invisible image of the Father, *the first begotten of every creature*—That is, begotten before every creature; subsisting before all worlds, before all time, from all eternity. (ENNT)

He Is the Firstborn over All Creation (Col. 1:15–17)

The word **firstborn** (v. 15) does not mean Christ was born to the Father. Firstborn often referred to a position of responsibility and authority in a family. The most favored son would receive the largest portion of the father's estate in order to care for the rest of the family. This birthright traditionally went to the eldest son, but not always (Gen. 25:29–34). This honor gave power and authority to the firstborn. God promised to appoint the Messiah His firstborn and to make Him "the most exalted of the kings of the earth" (Ps. 89:27). So when Paul wrote that Christ is **the firstborn over all creation** he was not saying Jesus was God's first creation. Paul meant that Christ holds the highest, most powerful, and most honored position in creation.

The word **for** introduces a list of reasons to believe Christ is **the firstborn over all creation**. Paul began by saying **all things were created** (Col. 1:16) by Christ. Some Greek philosophers thought God was too holy to have any contact with creation. They said He delegated the work of creation to angels. But Paul insisted that Christ created **all things . . . in heaven and on earth** (v. 16). He had contact with every part of creation, whether **visible** (physical) or **invisible** (spiritual).

Those who made the angels the agents of creation grouped them according to their power and authority. The angels were classified as **thrones or powers or rulers or authorities** (v. 16). Paul declared these levels of spiritual beings irrelevant because Christ made them all. In fact, **all things were created by him and for him** (v. 16). His words echo heaven's worship recorded in the book of Revelation. "You are worthy, our Lord and God, to receive glory and honor and power, for you created all things, and by your will they were created and have their being" (Rev. 4:11). Creation exists because of Christ's actions and for Him. He is both the originator and the reason for the universe's being.

He is before all things (Col. 1:17) because He is God, their Creator. John wrote, "In the beginning was the Word, and the Word was with God, and the Word was God. . . . Through him all things were made; without him nothing was made that has been made" (John 1:1, 3). **In him all things hold together** (Col. 1:17)—all the forces and laws of the cosmos are an expression of His power and mind. Therefore, the Christ that some said was an inadequate means of reaching God is source of all things, reason for all things, and power maintaining all things.

WORDS FROM WESLEY
Colossians 1:17

And he is before all things—It is not said, He was: He is from everlasting to everlasting. *And by him all things consist*—The original expression not only implies, that He sustains all things in being, but more directly, *All things were and are compacted in him into one system.* He is the cement as well as support of the universe. And is He less than the supreme God? (ENNT)

He Is the Head of the Body, the Church (Col. 1:18)

And—not only is Christ superior to all creation—**he is the head of . . . the church** (v. 18). Paul left the lofty regions of the universe and came down to the everyday lives of ordinary men and women. Christ is **the head of the body** (v. 18). He is connected to each and every believer because they are part of the church. However, a believer can lose connection with the Head by pursuing false teachings and worshiping angels (2:16–19).

Christ is the head (the source and supreme authority) of the church because **he is the beginning** (1:18). Just as Christ created the cosmos, He has created the church. He is **the firstborn from among the dead** (v. 18)—the first person to die and to leave the grave alive forever (Rev. 1:18).

Why did God work in and through Christ like this? **So that in everything** Christ **might have the supremacy** (Col. 1:18). Jesus has first place in heaven, on earth, in all creation, and in the church. He rules over the angelic beings the false teachers wanted to worship. Christ has the supremacy in every way. There is no need to add any religious rituals or philosophical ideas to Him. He is all we need to reach God.

WORDS FROM WESLEY
Colossians 1:18

And—From the whole, He now descends to the most eminent part, the church, *He is the head of the church*—Universal. The supreme and only head both of influence and of government to the whole body of believers, . . . *the beginning*—Absolutely the eternal, *the first-begotten from the dead*—From whose resurrection flows all the life, spiritual and eternal, of all His brethren: *that in all things*—Whether of nature or grace, *He might have the pre-eminence.* Who can sound this depth? (ENNT)

God Was Pleased to Have All His Fullness Dwell in Him (Col. 1:19–20)

Christ has first place in all things **for God was pleased to have all his fullness dwell in him** (v. 19). God was not coerced or persuaded to do this. God was pleased to become flesh and to live among us (John 1:14). Some Christians have tended to view God as an angry judge looking for any feasible excuse to punish human beings. They think we are fortunate because Christ stepped in to pacify God's anger by dying in our place. These Christians look at God the Father as a reluctant forgiver. But Paul made it very clear that **God was pleased to . . . reconcile** us **to himself** (vv. 19–20).

Not only was God pleased to participate in our salvation, but **all of his fullness** (v. 19) was in Christ. **Fullness** implies the very essence of what makes God divine. In other words, everything that makes Him God dwells in Christ. Believers don't need secret knowledge and angelic assistance to experience the fullness of God. We have it already in Christ alone.

God was pleased . . . to reconcile to himself all things (vv. 19–20) through Christ. It does not matter **whether** they are **things on earth** (physical) **or things in heaven** (spiritual). God made **peace through** Christ's **blood, shed on the cross** (v. 20). All of creation has been made right with God through Jesus Christ.

Christ in You, the Hope of Glory (Col. 1:27)

God's work of reconciliation not only affects all things; it has changed all believers. Although we were once alienated from God, we have been reconciled to Him through Jesus' sacrifice on the cross. We must continue in our "faith, established and firm, not moved from the hope held out in the gospel" (1:23). This is a significant warning to the Colossians who were leaving the gospel for something else.

Paul had been given a ministry to preach Christ's gospel to the world. The gospel was a mystery until God's Holy Spirit revealed it to the saints (1:24–26). No one could have expected that all kinds of persons could find God in one person (3:11).

But now, **to them** (the saints) **God has chosen to make known among the Gentiles the glorious riches of this mystery** (1:27). People all over the world were hearing the gospel (1:6, 23). The mystery reveals that all the glorious riches of God can belong to all of us because **Christ** is in us. He is our **hope of glory** (v. 27). Any human being who truly wants to find God can do so through Christ. And in Christ any human being can experience all the fullness of God (2:9).

WORDS FROM WESLEY

Colossians 1:27

The mystery so long unknown
Is manifest in Christ alone:
The fulness of the Deity
Resides eternally in Thee:
Jesus, to me the secret tell,
Thyself, the Gift unspeakable,
The hope of heavenly bliss impart,
The glorious earnest in my heart. (PW, vol. 13, 84)

DISCUSSION

Are you concerned that many individuals perceive Jesus as simply a cartoon figure, a superstar, a revolutionary, or merely a wonderful human being? Of course, none of these perceptions are correct. We must understand from Scripture who Jesus is in order to worship and serve Him correctly.

1. A false interpretation of "firstborn" in Colossians 1:15 suggests Jesus was the first one born at the time of creation. What is the correct meaning of "firstborn" as it applies to Jesus in Colossians 1:15?

2. What kind of worship should believers offer Jesus Christ in view of His preeminence? What kind of service should believers offer Him?

3. How does it affect your life to know Jesus hold all things together?

4. Why did Jesus have to be who He was in order to do what He did for you on the cross?

5. Far Eastern religion often depicts God as the soul of the universe. How would you respond to that concept of God?

6. How are you encouraged by the fact that Jesus is the Head of the church?

7. What unique factor about Christ's resurrection makes Him "the firstborn from the dead"?

8. How did Jesus reconcile you to God? What appropriate response to this reconciliation will you offer?

9. Why do you agree or disagree that unless Jesus is Lord of everything in a person's life, He is not Lord at all?

PRAYER

God give us a vision of the invisible power that is behind all things; and may we shape our lives and world by the knowledge that Christ reigns over everything. Amen.

12

FORGIVENESS

Philemon 1–25

God gives power to heal the impossibly broken relationships.

When we think we can never forgive a person who has wronged us, we need to ponder God's forgiveness. We had wronged Him by sinning. Our sins, like long, sharp nails, put Jesus on the cross. However, His love and desire to gain our forgiveness kept Him on the cross. Therefore, we are debtors to Him for the wonderful forgiveness we enjoy. But God expects us to forgive our offenders even as Christ forgave us (Col. 3:13).

This study examines Paul's appeal to Philemon to forgive a runaway slave who had become a believer. As you study this appeal, you will learn how to forgive as Christ forgave you.

COMMENTARY

The letter to Philemon is unique in the writings of Paul. It is very brief and deals with a single theme—the return of the slave Onesimus to his master Philemon. Onesimus had apparently run away from Colosse and made his way to Rome. (These comments assume that is the location where Paul was imprisoned at this writing.) In Rome, Onesimus came into contact with Paul and became a Christian believer. Evidently he was with Paul in Rome for an extended period, and they became close friends as well as Christian brothers.

In Colossians, Onesimus was traveling with Tychicus, the courier responsible for delivering the Colossian letter (4:7–9). This fact and other common references to persons makes it clear that

Colossians and Philemon were written and sent at the same time. Further evidence in Colossians and Ephesians makes it appear that the letter to the Ephesians also was delivered by Tychicus at the same time. The letter to the Colossians refers to Onesimus as "one of you" (4:9), so it is clear that Onesimus and Philemon were residents of Colosse.

What should a runaway slave do after becoming a Christian? This question is the central concern of the letter to Philemon. At least in this situation, Paul decided that Onesimus should return to his master, Philemon, who was also a Christian. Therefore, Onesimus was returning home, bringing this letter to his master. What would happen to him? Roman law allowed capital punishment for runaway slaves, so it was no light matter that Onesimus was going home to face the consequences of his actions.

WORDS FROM WESLEY

Philemon 1

This single epistle infinitely transcends all the wisdom of the world. And it gives us a specimen, how Christians ought to treat of secular affairs from higher principles. (ENNT)

Slavery was widespread in the Roman Empire. Perhaps one-third the population was made up of slaves. Slavery was the engine that drove the empire, and it was important to the Roman economic and cultural system that slavery be maintained. For that reason, slaves who ran away were perceived as a great threat to the empire, and the penalty for running away was severe. Philemon and other passages from Paul's writings, such as Colossians 3:22—4:1 and Ephesians 6:5–9, may be interpreted as approving of slavery. However, Paul gave clear orders to masters to treat their slaves kindly in the fear of God, their common Master.

Colossians 4:9 and Philemon 16 go further, calling Onesimus a Christian brother. In this thought, we see the beginning of the demise of slavery among Christians.

Though the letter to Philemon is short, it is a profound treatise on human relationships. It is fruitful to ponder its implications for us today as we consider employer-employee relationships.

Greetings (Philem. 1–3)

The letter was sent from Paul and his Christian brother Timothy. Paul characterized his status as that of **a prisoner of Christ Jesus (v. 1)**. It was sent to **Philemon our dear friend and fellow worker, to Apphia our sister, to Archippus our fellow soldier and to the church that meets in your home** (vv. 1–2). From verse 2, we learn that Paul considered Philemon a dear friend and a fellow worker in the work of Christ, and Apphia was probably Philemon's wife. Archippus was surely another minister of the church, and there was a church that met in Philemon's home.

WORDS FROM WESLEY

Philemon 2

As, "where two or three are met together in his name," there is Christ; so (to speak with St. Cyprian), "where two or three believers are met together, there is a church." Thus it is that St. Paul, writing to Philemon, mentions "the church which was in his house"; plainly signifying, that even a Christian family may be termed a church. (WJW, vol. 6, 392)

Grace to you and peace from God our Father and the Lord Jesus Christ (v. 3). This initial blessing is typical of Paul's letters. What greater wish can there be than grace (unmerited favor) and peace (absence of turmoil) from God?

Thanksgiving, Prayer, and Encouragement (Philem. 4–7)

Usually in his letters, Paul strongly affirmed the believers to whom he wrote. Note the phrases: **I always thank my God as I remember you in my prayers** (v. 4); **I hear about your faith in the Lord Jesus and your love for all the saints** (v. 5); **Your love has given me great joy and encouragement, because you, brother, have refreshed the hearts of the saints** (v. 7). Surely the tone of this passage would be encouraging to Philemon and others who read or heard it.

It seems certain that Philemon was a sincere believer who lived out his faith. His love for the saints was given concrete expression, refreshing their hearts. Philemon may have been fairly well to do, for he owned at least one slave and hosted a church in his home. Apparently he used his material blessings for the benefit of other believers. Paul had never visited Colosse, but he had heard of Philemon's generosity. That generosity caused Paul to rejoice and gave him encouragement.

Verse 6 is Paul's prayer for Philemon: **that you may be active in sharing your faith, so that you will have a full understanding of every good thing we have in Christ.** It appears that a full understanding of all the good things we have in Christ comes from actively sharing our faith.

A Plea for Onesimus (Philem. 8–11)

Paul could have used his personal prerogative, demanding that Philemon be kind to Onesimus, but instead he chose to **appeal to** him **on the basis of love** (v. 9). He used several persuasive devices, referring to what Philemon **ought to do** (v. 8), to the fact he (Paul) was **an old man and now also a prisoner of Christ Jesus** (v. 9). He called Onesimus his son **who became** his **son while** he **was in chains** (v. 10). Paul even used a play on words as part of his persuasion. The word *Onesimus* means useful, so verse 11 might be reworded: "Formerly he was not Onesimus to you, but now he has become Onesimus both to you and to me."

It is clear that Paul wanted Philemon to treat Onesimus with kindness and love. After all, Onesimus was agreeing to return to his master to settle past wrongs.

WORDS FROM WESLEY

Philemon 9

Yet out of love I rather entreat thee—In how handsome a manner does the apostle just hint, and immediately drop the consideration of his power to command, and tenderly entreat Philemon, to hearken to his friend, his aged friend, and now prisoner for Christ! With what endearment, in the next verse, does he call Onesimus his son, before he names his name! And as soon as he had mentioned it, with what fine address, does he just touch on his former faults, and instantly pass on to the happy change that was now made upon him! So disposing Philemon to attend to his request, and the motives wherewith he was going to enforce it. (ENNT)

Paul's Preference (Philem. 12–16)

Paul really wanted to keep Onesimus with him in Rome (v. 13). But Paul was sending his **very heart** back to Philemon (v. 12). Onesimus **could take** Philemon's **place in helping** Paul **while** he was **in chains. . . . But** he **did not want to do anything without** Philemon's **consent** (vv. 13–14). Paul would have liked to encourage Onesimus to stay in Rome, but he felt morally obligated to send him back to Philemon to make amends first. Following amends, Paul would obviously be delighted if Philemon would allow Onesimus to return to Rome.

As an illustration of Romans 8:28, Paul suggested that Onesimus had been **separated** from Philemon **for a little while . . . that** he **might have him back for good—no longer as a slave, but better than a slave, as a dear brother** (Philem. 15–16).

How wonderful that God had transformed the rebellious slave into a Christian brother.

Whether Paul favored slavery or not, any organized opposition to slavery could be extremely damaging to public opinion of Christianity. Strategically, Paul lived in a time when the church had to choose its cause carefully. Humane treatment of slaves was clearly required (Col. 4:1). Here Paul took another crucial step in the eventual elimination of slavery; he called Onesimus and Philemon "brothers." Paul also appealed to Philemon's Christian sensibilities. **He is very dear to me but even dearer to you, both as a man and as a brother in the Lord** (Philem. 16). Christian love would lead Philemon to do the right thing as he opened his heart to his repentant slave.

A Second Plea (Philem. 17-21)

Paul became very personal, laying his relationship with Philemon on the line. **If you consider me a partner, welcome him as you would welcome me** (v. 17). The great apostle asked that Philemon treat the slave as if he were Paul. Onesimus may have stolen money or valuables from Philemon, for Paul promised full payment of any debt. That was regardless of the fact that Philemon was indebted to Paul for his **very self** (v. 19). Though Paul had not visited Colosse personally, his representatives had no doubt founded the church and led Philemon to Christ.

WORDS FROM WESLEY

Philemon 17

If thou accountest me a partner—So that thy things are mine, and mine are thine. (ENNT)

I do wish, brother, that I may have some benefit from you in the Lord; refresh my heart in Christ (v. 20). Though he was not explicit, Paul seemingly returned to his earlier request that Onesimus be sent back to Rome as a companion for the apostle. There could hardly be any greater refreshment to Paul's heart than the companionship of a dear friend.

Paul ended his request with a statement of his confidence in Philemon, expecting him to **do even more than I ask** (v. 21). We do not know the outcome of this letter, but its place in the Canon surely implies it was successful, not disappointing Paul.

A Personal Request (Philem. 22)

Paul's optimism was evident: **Prepare a guest room for me, because I hope to be restored to you** (v. 22). Indeed, many scholars believe Paul was released from this imprisonment and that he traveled widely, possibly even to Spain, before he was imprisoned again and then executed under Nero. It is possible he made it to Colosse to enjoy Philemon's hospitality.

Final Greetings and Benediction (Philem. 23–25)

In verses 23 and 24, Paul mentioned several companions who sent greetings. **Epaphras**, who was described as a **fellow prisoner**, sent his greetings. Probably **fellow prisoner** should be taken in a spiritual sense. Compare Colossians 4:10, where Aristarchus was described as a fellow prisoner; and 4:12, where Epaphras was not. **Mark, Aristarchus, Demas and Luke** also sent greetings. These four are described as Paul's **fellow workers** (Philem. 24).

In typical fashion Paul closed this short letter with a blessing. His benediction was a simple but a profound wish: **The grace of the Lord Jesus Christ be with your spirit** (v. 25). Can anyone hope for anything greater than the grace of our Lord? Thus ended Paul's plea for his friend Onesimus.

DISCUSSION

It isn't always easy to forgive, and it's even harder to forgive and forget. Nevertheless, Paul implored Philemon to forgive someone who had wronged him.

1. What broken relationship did Paul address in his letter to Philemon?

2. What broken relationships, if any, would you like to see mended? What role might you play in mending these broken relationships?

3. Does it seem to you that Philemon's home was dedicated to the Lord? How might you use your home to serve the Lord?

4. Using fewer than five adjectives, how would you describe the forgiveness Christ has extended to you?

5. What commendable qualities and actions did Paul commend in Philemon?

6. What changes had Christ made in Onesimus's life? In your life?

7. Philemon's social status and Onesimus's social status were poles apart, and yet Paul said they were brothers in the Lord. How can the gospel embrace people of vastly different social or economic levels and make them brothers?

8. Should Christians forgive an offender unconditionally, or should we forgive only if the offender meets certain conditions? Is Jesus' forgiveness conditional or unconditional?

PRAYER

Lord Jesus, we find it hard to forgive as You have forgiven us. Help us to treat others with the same mercy and kindness with which You have shown us. May we live as people who have been bought with a price.

WORDS FROM WESLEY WORKS CITED

ENNT: *Explanatory Notes upon the New Testament,* by John Wesley, M.A. Fourth American Edition. New York: J. Soule and T. Mason, for the Methodist Episcopal Church in the United States, 1818.

PW: *The Poetical Works of John and Charles Wesley.* Edited by D. D. G. Osborn. 13 vols. London: Wesleyan-Methodist Conference Office, 1868.

WJW: *The Works of John Wesley.* Third Edition, Complete and Unabridged. 14 vols. London: Wesleyan Methodist Book Room, 1872.

OTHER BOOKS IN THE
WESLEY BIBLE STUDIES SERIES

Now Available in the
Wesley Bible Studies Series

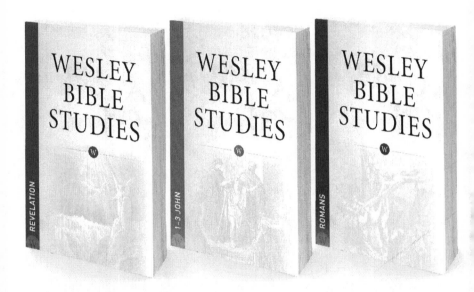

Each book in the Wesley Bible Studies series provides a thoughtful and powerful survey of key Scriptures in one or more biblical books. They combine accessible commentary from contemporary teachers, with relevantly highlighted direct quotes from the complete writings and life experiences of John Wesley, along with the poetry and hymns of his brother Charles. For each study, creative and engaging questions foster deeper fellowship and growth.

<table>
<tr><td align="center">Revelation
978-0-89827-878-1
978-0-89827-879-8 (e-book)</td><td align="center">Romans
978-0-89827-854-5
978-0-89827-855-2 (e-book)</td></tr>
</table>

1–3 John
978-0-89827-856-9
978-0-89827-857-6 (e-book)

1.800.493.7539   wphstore.com